Oracle PL/SQL Language
Pocket Reference

Oracle PL/SQL Language
Pocket Reference

Steven Feuerstein,
Bill Pribyl, and Chip Dawes

O'REILLY®

Beijing • Cambridge • Köln • Paris • Sebastopol • Taipei • Tokyo

Oracle PL/SQL Language Pocket Reference

by Steven Feuerstein, Bill Pribyl, and Chip Dawes

Copyright © 1999 O'Reilly & Associates, Inc. All rights reserved.
Printed in the United States of America.
Published by O'Reilly & Associates, Inc., 101 Morris Street,
Sebastopol, CA 95472.

Editors: Gigi Estabrook and Deborah Russell

Production Editor: Sarah Jane Shangraw

Cover Design: Edie Freedman

Printing History:

April 1999:   First Edition.

1-56592-457-6

Table of Contents

Oracle PL/SQL Language Pocket Reference

Introduction

The *Oracle PL/SQL Language Pocket Reference* is a quick reference guide to the PL/SQL programming language, which provides procedural extensions to the SQL relational database language and a range of Oracle development tools.

Where a package, program, or function is supported only for a particular version of Oracle (e.g., Oracle8*i*), we indicate this in the text.

The purpose of this pocket reference is to help PL/SQL users find the syntax of specific language elements. It is not a self-contained user guide; basic knowledge of the PL/SQL programming language is required. For more information, see the following books:

Oracle PL/SQL Programming, Second Edition, by Steven Feuerstein with Bill Pribyl (O'Reilly & Associates, 1997).

Oracle Built-in Packages, by Steven Feuerstein, Charles Dye, and John Beresniewicz (O'Reilly & Associates, 1998).

Oracle PL/SQL Built-ins Pocket Reference, by Steven Feuerstein, John Beresniewicz, and Chip Dawes (O'Reilly & Associates, 1998).

Acknowledgments

We would like to thank our reviewers: Eric J. Givler, Department of Environmental Protection, Harrisburg, Pennsylvania; and Stephen Nelson, HK Systems, New Berlin, Wisconsin.

Conventions

UPPERCASE indicates PL/SQL keywords.

lowercase indicates user-defined items such as parameters.

Italic indicates file names and parameters within text.

`Constant width` is used for code examples.

[] enclose optional items in syntax descriptions.

{} enclose a list of items in syntax descriptions; you must choose one item from the list.

| separates bracketed list items in syntax descriptions.

PL/SQL Language Fundamentals

The PL/SQL Character Set

The PL/SQL language is constructed from letters, digits, symbols, and whitespace, as defined in the following table.

Type	Characters
Letters	`A-Z, a-z`
Digits	`0-9`
Symbols	`~!@#$%&*()_-+=|[]{}:;"'<>?/`
Whitespace	space, tab, carriage return

Characters are grouped together into the four lexical units: identifiers, literals, delimiters, and comments.

Identifiers

Identifiers are names for PL/SQL objects such as constants, variables, exceptions, procedures, cursors, and reserved words. Identifiers:

- Can be up to 30 characters in length
- Cannot include whitespace (space, tab, carriage return)
- Must start with a letter
- Can include a dollar sign ($), an underscore (_), and a pound sign (#)
- Are not case-sensitive

If you enclose an identifier within double quotes, then all but the first of these rules are ignored. For example, the following declaration is valid:

```
DECLARE
   "1 ^abc"  VARCHAR2(100);
BEGIN
   IF "1 ^abc" IS NULL THEN ...
END;
```

Literals

Literals are specific values not represented by identifiers. For example, TRUE, 3.14159, 6.63E-34, 'Moby Dick', and NULL are all literals of type Boolean, number, or string. There are no date or complex datatype literals as they are internal representations. Unlike the rest of PL/SQL, literals are case-sensitive. To embed single quotes within a string literal, place two single quotes next to each other. See the following table for examples.

Literal	Actual Value
'That''s Entertainment!'	That's Entertainment!
'"The Raven"'	"The Raven"
'TZ="CDT6CST"'	TZ='CDT6CST'
''''	'

Literal	Actual Value
`'''hello world'''`	`'hello world'`
`''''''`	`''`

Delimiters

Delimiters are symbols with special meaning, such as :=
(assignment operator), || (concatenation operator), and ;
(statement delimiter). The following table lists delimiters.

Delimiter	Description
`;`	Statement terminator
`+`	Addition operator
`-`	Subtraction operator
`*`	Multiplication operator
`/`	Division operator
`**`	Exponentiation operator
`||`	Concatenation operator
`:=`	Assignment operator
`=`	Equality operator
`<>` and `!=`	Inequality operators
`^=` and `~=`	Inequality operators
`<`	"Less than" operator
`<=`	"Less than or equal to" operator
`>`	"Greater than" operator
`>=`	"Greater than or equal to" operator
`(` and `)`	Expression or list delimiters
`<<` and `>>`	Label delimiters
`,`	Item separator
`'`	Literal delimiter
`"`	Quoted literal delimiter
`:`	Host variable indicator
`%`	Attribute indicator

Delimiter	Description
.	Component indicator (as in record.field or package.element)
@	Remote database indicator (database link)
=>	Association operator (named notation)
..	Range operator (used in the FOR loop)
--	Single-line comment indicator
/* and */	Multiline comment delimiters

Comments

Comments are sections of the code that exist to aid readability. The compiler ignores them.

A single-line comment begins with a double hyphen (--) and ends with a new line. The compiler ignores all characters between the -- and the new line.

Multiline comments begin with slash asterisk (/*) and end with asterisk slash (*/). The /* */ comment delimiters can also be used on a single-line comment. The following block demonstrates both kinds of comments:

```
DECLARE
    -- Two dashes comment out only the physical line.
    /* Everything is a comment until the compiler
       encounters the following symbol */
```

You cannot embed multiline comments within a multiline comment, so care needs to be exercised during development if you comment out portions of code that include comments. The following code demonstrates:

```
DECLARE
    /* Everything is a comment until the compiler
    /* This comment inside another WON'T work!*/
       encounters the following symbol. */

    /* Everything is a comment until the compiler
       -- This comment inside another WILL work!
       encounters the following symbol. */
```

Pragmas

The PRAGMA keyword is used to give instructions to the compiler. There are four types of pragmas in PL/SQL:

EXCEPTION_INIT

Tells the compiler to associate the specified error number with an identifier that has been declared an EXCEPTION in your current program or an accessible package. See the "Exception Handling" section for more information on this pragma.

RESTRICT_REFERENCES

Tells the compiler the purity level of a packaged program. The purity level is the degree to which a program does not read/write database tables and/or package variables. See the "Calling PL/SQL Functions in SQL" section for more information on this pragma.

SERIALLY_REUSABLE

Tells the runtime engine that package data should not persist between references. This is used to reduce per-user memory requirements when the package data is only needed for the duration of the call and not for the duration of the session. See the "Packages" section for more information on this pragma.

AUTONOMOUS_TRANSACTION (Oracle8i)

Tells the compiler that the function, procedure, top-level anonymous PL/SQL block, object method, or database trigger executes in its own transaction space. See the "Database Interaction and Cursors" section for more information on this pragma.

Statements

A PL/SQL program is composed of one or more logical statements. A statement is terminated by a semicolon delimiter. The physical end-of-line marker in a PL/SQL program is ignored by the compiler, except to terminate a single-line comment (initiated by the -- symbol).

Block structure

Each PL/SQL program is a block consisting of a standard set of elements, identified by keywords (see Figure 1). The block determines the scope of declared elements, and how exceptions are handled and propagated. A block can be anonymous or named. Named blocks include functions, procedures, packages, and triggers. Here is an example of an anonymous block:

```
DECLARE
    whoops NUMBER DEFAULT 99;
BEGIN
    -- Display a two-digit year number.
    DBMS_OUTPUT.PUT_LINE ('What century?' || whoops);
END;
```

Here is a named block that performs the same action:

```
CREATE OR REPLACE PROCEDURE show_the_problem
IS
    whoops NUMBER DEFAULT 99;
BEGIN
    -- Display a two-digit year number.
    DBMS_OUTPUT.PUT_LINE ('What century?' || whoops);
END show_the_problem;
```

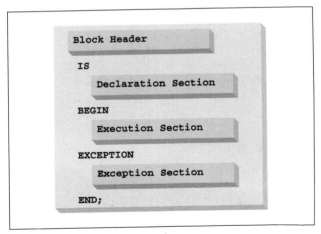

Figure 1. The PL/SQL block structure

The following table describes the sections of a PL/SQL block:

Section	Description
Header	Required for named blocks. Specifies the way the program is called by outer PL/SQL blocks. Anonymous blocks do not have a header. They start with the DECLARE keyword if there is a declaration section, or with the BEGIN keyword if there are no declarations.
Declaration	Optional; declares variables, cursors, TYPEs, and local programs that are used in the block's execution and exception sections.
Execution	Optional in package and type specifications; contains statements that are executed when the block is run.
Exception	Optional; describes error handling behavior for exceptions raised in the executable section.

Variables and Program Data

PL/SQL programs are normally used to manipulate database information. You commonly do this by declaring variables and data structures in your programs, and then working with that PL/SQL-specific data.

A variable is a named instantiation of a data structure declared in a PL/SQL block (either locally or in a package). Unless you declare a variable as a CONSTANT, its value can be changed at any time in your program.

The following table describes several types of program data.

Type	Description
Scalar	Variables made up of a single value, such as a number, date, or Boolean.
Composite	Variables made up of multiple values, such as a record or collection.
Reference	Pointers to values.
LOB	Variables containing Large OBject (LOB) locators.

Scalar Datatypes

Scalar datatypes divide into four families: number, character, date-time, and Boolean.

Numeric datatypes

Numeric datatypes are further divided into decimal, binary integer, and PLS_INTEGER storage types.

Decimal numeric datatypes store fixed and floating-point numbers of just about any size. They include NUMBER, DEC, DECIMAL, NUMERIC, FLOAT, REAL, and DOUBLE PRECISION. The maximum precision of a variable with type NUMBER is 38 digits, which yields a range of values from 1.0E–129 through 9.999E125. This range of numbers would include the mass of an electron over the mass of the universe or the size of the universe in angstroms.

Variables of type NUMBER can be declared with precision and scale, as follows:

```
NUMBER(precision, scale)
```

Precision is the number of digits, and scale denotes the number of digits to the right (positive scale) or left (negative scale) of the decimal point at which rounding occurs. Legal values for the scale range from –84 to 127. The following table shows examples of precision and scale.

Declaration	Assigned Value	Stored Value
NUMBER	6.02	6.02
NUMBER(4)	8675	8675
NUMBER(4)	8675309	Error
NUMBER(12,5)	3.14159265	3.14159
NUMBER(12,–5)	8675309	8700000

Binary integer numeric datatypes store whole numbers. They include BINARY_INTEGER, INTEGER, INT, SMALLINT, NATURAL, NATURALN, POSITIVE, POSITIVEN, and

SIGNTYPE. Binary integer datatypes store signed integers in the range of $-2^{31} + 1$ to $2^{31} - 1$. The subtypes include NATURAL (0 through 2^{31}) and POSITIVE (1 through 2^{31}) together with the NOT NULL variations NATURALN and POSITIVEN. SIGNTYPE is restricted to three values (-1, 0, 1).

PLS_INTEGER datatypes have the same range as the BINARY_INTEGER datatype, but use machine arithmetic instead of library arithmetic, so are slightly faster for computation-heavy processing.

The following table lists the PL/SQL numeric datatypes with ANSI and IBM compatibility.

PL/SQL Datatype	Compatibility	Oracle RDNMS Datatype
DEC(prec,scale)	ANSI	NUMBER(prec,scale)
DECIMAL(prec,scale)	IBM	NUMBER(prec,scale)
DOUBLE PRECISION	ANSI	NUMBER
FLOAT(binary)	ANSI, IBM	NUMBER
INT	ANSI	NUMBER(38)
INTEGER	ANSI, IBM	NUMBER(38)
NUMERIC(prec,scale)	ANSI	NUMBER(prec,scale)
REAL	ANSI	NUMBER
SMALLINT	ANSI, IBM	NUMBER(38)

In the preceding table:

- *prec* is the precision for the subtype.
- *scale* is the scale of the subtype.
- *binary* is the binary precision of the subtype.

Character datatypes

Character datatypes store alphanumeric text and are manipulated by character functions. As with the numeric family, there are several subtypes in the character family, shown in the following table.

Family	Description
CHAR	Fixed-length alphanumeric strings. Valid sizes are 1 to 32767 bytes (which is larger than the Oracle7 limit of 2000 and the Oracle8 limit of 4000).
VARCHAR2	Variable-length alphanumeric strings. Valid sizes are 1 to 32767 bytes (which is larger than the Oracle7 limit of 2000 and the Oracle8 limit of 4000).
LONG	Variable-length alphanumeric strings. Valid sizes are 1 to 32760 bytes. LONG is included primarily for backward compatibility since longer strings can now be stored in VARCHAR2 variables.
RAW	Variable-length binary strings. Valid sizes are 1 to 32767 bytes (which is larger than the Oracle7 and Oracle8 limit of 2000). RAW data do not undergo character set conversion when selected from a remote database.
LONG RAW	Variable-length binary strings. Valid sizes are 1 to 32760 bytes. LONG RAW is included primarily for backward compatibility since longer strings can now be stored in RAW variables.

ROWID	Fixed-length binary data. Every row in a database has a physical address or ROWID. An Oracle7 (restricted) ROWID has 3 parts in base 16 (hex):
	    BBBBBBBB.RRRR.FFFF.
	An Oracle8 (extended) ROWID has 4 parts in base 64:
	    OOOOOOFFFBBBBBBRRR.
	where:
	    OOOOOO is the object number.
	    FFFF (FFF) is the absolute (Oracle 7) or relative (Oracle8) file number.
	    BBBBBBBB (BBBBBB) is the block number within the file.
	    RRRR (RRR) is the row number within the block.

UROWID (Oracle8*i*)	Universal ROWID. Variable-length hexadecimal string depicting a logical ROWID. Valid sizes are up to 4000 bytes. Used to store the addresses of rows in index organized tables or IBM DB2 tables via Gateway.

Date-time datatypes

DATE values are fixed-length, date-plus-time values. The DATE datatype can store dates from January 1, 4712 B.C. to December 31, 4712 A.D. Each DATE includes the century, year, month, day, hour, minute, and second. Sub-second granularity is not supported via the DATE datatype. The time portion of a DATE defaults to midnight (12:00:00 AM) if it is not included explicitly. The internal calendar follows the Papal standard of Julian to Gregorian conversion in 1582 rather than the English standard (1752) found in many operating systems.

Boolean datatype

The BOOLEAN datatype can store one of only three values: TRUE, FALSE, or NULL. BOOLEAN variables are usually used in logical control structures such as IF…THEN or LOOP statements.

Following are truth tables showing the results of logical AND, OR, and NOT operations with PL/SQL's three-value Boolean model.

AND	TRUE	FALSE	NULL
TRUE	TRUE	FALSE	NULL
FALSE	FALSE	FALSE	FALSE
NULL	NULL	FALSE	NULL

OR	TRUE	FALSE	NULL
TRUE	TRUE	TRUE	TRUE
FALSE	TRUE	FALSE	NULL
NULL	TRUE	NULL	NULL

NOT (TRUE)	NOT (FALSE)	NOT (NULL)
FALSE	TRUE	NULL

NLS Character Datatypes

The standard ASCII character set does not support some languages, such as Chinese, Japanese, or Korean. To support these multibyte character sets, PL/SQL8 supports two character sets, the database character set and the national character set (NLS). There are two datatypes, NCHAR and NVARCHAR2, that can be used to store data in the national character set.

NCHAR values are fixed-length NLS character data; the maximum length is 32767 bytes. For variable-length character sets (like JA16SJIS), the length specification is in bytes; for fixed-length character sets, the it is in characters.

NVARCHAR2 values are variable-length NLS character data. The maximum length is 32767 bytes, and the length specification follows the same fixed/variable-length rule as NCHAR values.

LOB Datatypes

PL/SQL8 supports a number of Large OBject (LOB) datatypes, which can store objects of up to four gigabytes of data. Unlike the scalar datatypes, variables declared for LOBs use locators, or pointers to the actual data. LOBs are manipulated in PL/SQL using the built-in package DBMS_ LOB.

BFILE

File locators pointing to read-only large binary objects in operating system files. With BFILEs, the large objects are outside the database.

BLOB

LOB locators that point to large binary objects inside the database.

CLOB

LOB locators that point to large "character" (alphanumeric) objects inside the database.

NCLOB

LOB locators that point to large national character set objects inside the database.

NULLs in PL/SQL

PL/SQL represents unknown values as NULL values. Since a NULL is unknown, a NULL is never equal or not equal to anything (including another NULL value). Additionally, most functions return a NULL when passed a NULL argument—the notable exceptions are NVL, CONCAT, and REPLACE. You cannot check for equality or inequality to NULL; therefore, you must use the IS NULL or IS NOT NULL syntax to check for NULL values.

Here is an example of the IS NULL syntax to check the value of a variable:

```
BEGIN
   IF myvar IS NULL
   THEN
      ...
```

Declaring Variables

Before you can use a variable, you must first declare it in the declaration section of your PL/SQL block or in a package as a global. When you declare a variable, PL/SQL allocates memory for the variable's value and names the storage location so that the value can be retrieved and changed. The syntax for a variable declaration is:

```
variable_name datatype [CONSTANT] [NOT NULL]
   [:= | DEFAULT initial_value]
```

Constrained declarations

The datatype in a declaration can be constrained or unconstrained. Constrained datatypes have a size, scale, or precision limit that is less than the unconstrained datatype. For example:

```
total_sales      NUMBER(15,2);   -- Constrained.
emp_id           VARCHAR2(9);    -- Constrained.
company_number   NUMBER;         -- Unconstrained.
book_title       VARCHAR2;       -- Not valid.
```

Constrained declarations require less memory than uncon-strained declarations. Not all datatypes can be specified as unconstrained. You cannot, for example, declare a variable to be of type VARCHAR2. You must always specify the maximum size of a variable-length string.

Constants

The CONSTANT keyword in a declaration requires an ini-tial value and does not allow that value to be changed. For example:

```
min_order_qty    NUMBER(1) CONSTANT := 5;
```

Default values

Whenever you declare a variable, it is assigned a default val-ue of NULL. Initializing all variables is distinctive to PL/SQL; in this way, PL/SQL differs from languages such as C and Ada. If you want to initialize a variable to a value other than NULL, you do so in the declaration with either the assignment operator (:=) or the DEFAULT keyword:

```
counter    BINARY_INTEGER := 0;
priority   VARCHAR2(8)    DEFAULT 'LOW';
```

A NOT NULL constraint can be appended to the variable's datatype declaration to indicate that NULL is not a valid val-ue. If you add the NOT NULL constraint, you must explicitly assign an initial value for that variable.

Anchored Declarations

Use the %TYPE attribute to *anchor* the datatype of a scalar variable to either another variable or to a column in a data-base table or view. Use %ROWTYPE to anchor a record's declaration to a cursor or table (see the "Records in PL/SQL" section for more detail on the %ROWTYPE attribute).

The following block shows several variations of anchored declarations:

```
DECLARE
tot_sales NUMBER(20,2);
   -- Anchor to a PL/SQL variable.
   monthly_sales tot_sales%TYPE;

   -- Anchor to a database column.
   v_ename employee.last_name%TYPE;

   CURSOR mycur IS
      SELECT * FROM employee;

   -- Anchor to a cursor.
   myrec mycur%ROWTYPE;
```

The NOT NULL clause on a variable declaration (but not on a database column definition) follows the %TYPE anchoring and requires anchored declarations to have a default in their declaration. The default value for an anchored declaration can be different from that for the base declaration:

```
tot_sales      NUMBER(20,2) NOT NULL DEFAULT 0;
monthly_sales  tot_sales%TYPE DEFAULT 10;
```

Programmer-Defined Subtypes

PL/SQL allows you to define unconstrained scalar subtypes. An unconstrained subtype provides an alias to the original underlying datatype, for example:

```
CREATE OR REPLACE PACKAGE std_types
IS
   -- Declare standard types as globals.
   TYPE dollar_amt_t IS NUMBER;
END std_types;

CREATE OR REPLACE PROCEDURE process_money
IS
   -- Use the global type declared above.
   credit std_types.dollar_amt_t;
   ...
```

A constrained subtype limits or constrains the new datatype to a subset of the original datatype. For example, POSITIVE is a constrained subtype of BINARY_INTEGER. The declaration for POSITIVE in the STANDARD package is:

```
SUBTYPE POSITIVE IS BINARY_INTEGER RANGE
1..2147483647;
```

You cannot define constrained subtypes in your own programs; this capability is reserved for Oracle itself. You can, however, achieve the same effect as a constrained subtype by using %TYPE. Here is a rewriting of the previous subtype that enforces a constraint on the size of dollar amount variables:

```
PACKAGE std_types
IS
    v_dollar NUMBER (10, 2);

    TYPE dollar_amt_t IS v_dollar%TYPE;
END;
```

Conditional and Sequential Control

PL/SQL includes conditional (IF) structures as well as sequential control (GOTO, NULL) constructs.

Conditional Control Statements

IF-THEN combination

```
IF condition THEN
    executable statement(s)
END IF;
```

For example:

```
IF caller_type = 'VIP' THEN
    generate_response('GOLD');
END IF;
```

IF-THEN-ELSE combination

```
IF condition THEN
    TRUE sequence_of_executable_statement(s)
ELSE
    FALSE/NULL sequence_of_executable_statement(s)
END IF;
```

For example:

```
IF caller_type = 'VIP' THEN
   generate_response('GOLD');
ELSE
   generate_response('BRONZE');
END IF;
```

IF-THEN-ELSIF combination

```
IF condition-1 THEN
   statements-1
ELSIF condition-N THEN
   statements-N
[ELSE
   else statements]
END IF;
```

For example:

```
IF caller_type = 'VIP' THEN
   generate_response('GOLD');
ELSIF priority_client THEN
   generate_response('SILVER');
ELSE
   generate_response('BRONZE');
END IF;
```

Sequential Control Statements

The GOTO statement performs unconditional branching to a named label. It should be used rarely. At least one executable statement must follow the label (the NULL statement can be this necessary executable statement). The format of a GOTO statement is:

GOTO *label_name;*

The format of the label is:

<<label_name>>

There are a number of scope restrictions on where a GOTO can branch control. A GOTO:

- Can branch out of an IF statement, LOOP, or sub-block
- Cannot branch into an IF statement, LOOP, or sub-block

- Cannot branch from one section of an IF statement to another (from the IF/THEN section to the ELSE section is illegal)

- Cannot branch into or out of a subprogram

- Cannot branch from the exception section to the executable section of a PL/SQL block

- Cannot branch from the executable section to the exception section of a PL/SQL block, although a RAISE does this

The NULL statement is an executable statement that does nothing. It is useful when an executable statement must follow a GOTO label or to aid readability in an IF-THEN-ELSE structure. For example:

```
IF :report.selection = 'DETAIL' THEN
    exec_detail_report;
ELSE
    NULL;
END IF;
```

Loops

The LOOP construct allows you to repeatedly execute a sequence of statements. There are three kind of loops: simple, WHILE, and FOR.

Use the EXIT statement to break out of LOOP and pass control to the statement following the END LOOP.

The Simple Loop

The syntax for a simple loop is:

```
LOOP
    executable_statement(s)
END LOOP;
```

The simple loop should contain an EXIT or EXIT WHEN statement so as not to execute infinitely. Use the simple loop when you want the body of the loop to execute at least once.

For example:

```
LOOP
   FETCH company_cur INTO company_rec;
   EXIT WHEN company_cur%ROWCOUNT > 5 OR
      company_cur%NOTFOUND;
   process_company(company_cur);
END LOOP;
```

The Numeric FOR Loop

The syntax for a numeric FOR loop is:

```
FOR loop_index IN [REVERSE] lowest_number..
   highest_number
LOOP
   executable_statement(s)
END LOOP;
```

The PL/SQL runtime engine automatically declares the loop index a PLS_INTEGER variable; never declare a variable with that name yourself. The *lowest_number* and *highest_number* ranges can be variables, but are evaluated only once—on initial entry into the loop. The REVERSE keyword causes PL/SQL to start with the *highest_number* and decrement down to the *lowest_number*. For example:

```
BEGIN
   DBMS_OUTPUT.PUT_LINE('Beginning Forward');
   FOR counter IN 1 .. 4
   LOOP
      DBMS_OUTPUT.PUT_LINE('counter='||counter);
   END LOOP;

   DBMS_OUTPUT.PUT_LINE('Beginning REVERSE');
   FOR counter IN REVERSE 1 .. 4
   LOOP
      DBMS_OUTPUT.PUT_LINE('counter='||counter);
   END LOOP;
END;
```

The Cursor FOR Loop

The syntax for a cursor FOR loop is:

```
FOR record_index IN [cursor_name | SELECT statement]
LOOP
   executable_statement(s)
END LOOP;
```

The PL/SQL runtime engine automatically declares the loop index a record of *cursor_name*%ROWTYPE; never declare a variable with that name yourself.

The cursor FOR loop automatically opens the cursor, fetches all rows identified by the cursor, and then closes the cursor. You can embed the SELECT statement directly in the cursor FOR loop. For example:

```
FOR emp_rec IN emp_cur
LOOP
    IF emp_rec.title = 'Oracle Programmer'
    THEN
        give_raise(emp_rec.emp_id,30)
    END IF;
END LOOP;
```

The WHILE Loop

The syntax for a WHILE loop is:

```
WHILE condition
LOOP
    executable_statement(s)
END LOOP;
```

Use the WHILE loop when, depending on the entry condition, you don't want the loop body to execute even once:

```
WHILE NOT end_of_analysis
LOOP
    perform_analysis;
    get_next_record;
    IF analysis_cursor%NOTFOUND AND next_step IS NULL
    THEN
        end_of_analysis := TRUE;
    END IF;
END LOOP;
```

The REPEAT UNTIL Loop Emulation

PL/SQL does not directly support a REPEAT UNTIL construct, but a modified simple loop can emulate one. The syntax for this emulated REPEAT UNTIL loop is:

```
LOOP
    executable_statement(s)
    EXIT WHEN Boolean_condition;
END LOOP;
```

Use the emulated REPEAT UNTIL loop when executing iterations indefinitely before conditionally terminating the loop.

The EXIT Statement

The syntax for the EXIT statement is:

```
EXIT [WHEN Boolean_condition];
```

If you do not include a WHEN clause in the EXIT statement, it will terminate the loop unconditionally. Otherwise, the loop terminates only if *Boolean_condition* evaluates to TRUE. The EXIT statement is optional and can appear anywhere in the loop.

Loop Labels

Loops can be optionally labeled to improve readability and execution control. The label must appear immediately in front of the statement that initiates the loop.

The following example demonstrates the use of loop labels to qualify variables within a loop and also to terminate nested and outer loops:

```
<<year_loop>>
FOR yearind IN 1 .. 20
LOOP
    <<month_loop>>
    LOOP
        ...
        IF year_loop.yearind > 10
        THEN
            EXIT year_loop;
        END IF;
    END LOOP month_loop;
END LOOP year_loop;
```

Database Interaction and Cursors

PL/SQL is tightly integrated with the underlying SQL layer of the Oracle database. You can execute SQL statements (UPDATE, INSERT, DELETE, and SELECT) directly in PL/SQL programs. You can also execute Data Definition Language (DDL) statements through the use of dynamic SQL (DBMS_SQL in Oracle7 and Oracle8, native dynamic SQL in Oracle8*i*). In addition, you can manage transactions with COMMIT, ROLLBACK, and other Data Control Language (DCL) statements.

Transaction Management

The Oracle RDBMS provides a transaction model based on a unit of work. The PL/SQL language supports most, but not all, of the database model for transactions (you cannot, for example, ROLLBACK FORCE). Transactions begin with the first change to data and end with either a COMMIT or ROLLBACK. Transactions are independent of PL/SQL blocks. Transactions can span multiple PL/SQL blocks, or there can be multiple transactions in a single PL/SQL block. The PL/SQL supported transaction statements are: COMMIT, ROLLBACK, SAVEPOINT, SET TRANSACTION, and LOCK TABLE. Each is detailed here:

COMMIT

```
COMMIT [WORK] [COMMENT text];
```

COMMIT makes the database changes permanent and visible to other database sessions. The WORK keyword is optional and only aids readability—it is rarely used. The COMMENT text is optional and can be up to 50 characters in length. It is only germane to in-doubt distributed (two-phase commit) transactions. The database statement COMMIT FORCE for distributed transactions is not supported in PL/SQL.

ROLLBACK

```
ROLLBACK [WORK] [TO [SAVEPOINT] savepoint_name];
```

ROLLBACK undoes the changes made in the current transaction either to the beginning of the transaction or to a *savepoint*. A savepoint is a named processing point in a

---

transaction, created with the SAVEPOINT statement. Rolling back to a savepoint is a partial rollback of a transaction, wiping out all changes (and savepoints) that occurred later than the named savepoint.

SAVEPOINT

```
SAVEPOINT savepoint_name;
```

SAVEPOINT establishes a savepoint in the current transaction. *savepoint_name* is an undeclared identifier—you do not declare it. More than one savepoint can be established within a transaction. If you reuse a savepoint name, that savepoint is *moved* to the later position and you will not be able to rollback to the initial savepoint position.

SET TRANSACTION

```
SET TRANSACTION READ ONLY;
SET TRANSACTION ISOLATION LEVEL SERIALIZABLE;
SET TRANSACTION USE ROLLBACK SEGMENT rbseg_name;
```

SET TRANSACTION has three transaction control functions:

READ ONLY

Marks the beginning of a read-only transaction. This indicates to the RDBMS that a read-consistent view of the database is to be enforced for the transaction (the default is for the statement). This read-consistent view means that only changes committed before the transaction begins are visible for the duration of the transaction. The transaction is ended with either a COMMIT or ROLLBACK. Only LOCK TABLE, SELECT, SELECT INTO, OPEN, FETCH, CLOSE, COMMIT, or ROLLBACK statements are permitted during a read-only transaction. Issuing other statements, such as INSERT or UPDATE, in a read-only transaction results in an ORA-1456 error.

ISOLATION LEVEL SERIALIZABLE

Similar to a READ ONLY transaction in that transaction-level read consistency is enforced instead of the default statement-level read consistency. Serializable transactions do allow changes to data, however.

USE ROLLBACK SEGMENT

Tells the RDBMS to use the specifically named rollback segment *rbseg_name*. This statement is useful when only one rollback segment is large and a program knows that it needs to use the large rollback segment, such as during a month-end close operation. For example, if we know our large rollback segment is named *rbs_large*, we can tell the database to use it by issuing the following statement before our first change to data:

```
SET TRANSACTION USE ROLLBACK SEGMENT rbs_large;
```

LOCK TABLE

```
LOCK TABLE table_list IN lock_mode MODE [NOWAIT];
```

This statement bypasses the implicit database row-level locks by explicitly locking one or more tables in the specified mode. The *table_list* is a comma-delimited list of tables. The *lock_mode* is one of ROW SHARE, ROW EXCLUSIVE, SHARE UPDATE, SHARE, SHARE ROW EXCLUSIVE, or EXCLUSIVE. The NOWAIT keyword specifies that the RDBMS should not wait for a lock to be released. If there is a lock when NOWAIT is specified, the RDBMS raises the exception "ORA-00054: resource busy and acquire with NOWAIT specified". The default RDBMS locking behavior is to wait indefinitely.

Native Dynamic SQL (Oracle8i)

Native dynamic SQL introduces a new PL/SQL statement, EXECUTE IMMEDIATE, and new semantics for the OPEN FOR, FETCH, and CLOSE statement family. The former applies to single-row queries and DDL, while the latter supports dynamic multi-row queries. The syntax for these statements is:

```
EXECUTE IMMEDIATE SQL_statement_string
[INTO { define_variable_list | record |
    object_variable }]
[USING [IN | OUT | IN OUT] bind_argument_list];
```

```
OPEN cursor_variable FOR
   SELECT_statement_string;

FETCH cursor_variable INTO {define_variable_list
   | record | object_variable};
CLOSE cursor_variable;
```

The EXECUTE IMMEDIATE statement parses and executes
the SQL statement in a single step. It can be used for any
SQL statement except a multi-row query. *define_variable_
list* is a comma-delimited list of variable names; the *bind_
argument_list* is a comma-delimited list of bind arguments.
The parameter mode is optional and defaults to IN. Do not
place a trailing semicolon in the *SQL_statement_string*.

This is the statement that can be used to execute DDL without the DBMS_SQL package. For example:

```
EXECUTE IMMEDIATE 'TRUNCATE TABLE foo';
EXECUTE IMMEDIATE 'GRANT SELECT ON '|| tabname_v ||
   ' TO ' || grantee_list;
```

The OPEN FOR statement assigns a multi-row query to a
weakly typed cursor variable. The rows are then FETCHed
and the cursor CLOSEd.

```
DECLARE
   TYPE cv_typ IS REF CURSOR;
   cv cv_typ;
   laccount_no NUMBER;
   lbalance NUMBER;
BEGIN
   OPEN cv FOR
      'SELECT account_no, balance
         FROM accounts
        WHERE balance < 500';
   LOOP
      FETCH cv INTO laccount_no, lbalance;
      EXIT WHEN cv%NOTFOUND;
      -- Process the row.
   END LOOP;
   CLOSE cv;
END;
```

Autonomous Transactions (Oracle8i)

Autonomous transactions execute within a block of code as
separate transactions from the outer (main) transaction.

Changes can be committed or rolled back in an autonomous transaction without committing or rolling back the main transaction. Changes committed in an autonomous transaction are visible to the main transaction, even though they occur after the start of the main transaction. Changes committed in an autonomous transaction are visible to other transactions as well. The RDBMS suspends the main transaction while the autonomous transaction executes:

```
PROCEDURE main IS
BEGIN
   UPDATE ...-- Main transaction begins here.
   DELETE ...
   at_proc;  -- Call the autonomous transaction.
   SELECT ...
   INSERT ...
   COMMIT;   -- Main transaction ends here.
END;

PROCEDURE at_proc IS
   PRAGMA AUTONOMOUS_TRANSACTION;
BEGIN          -- Main transaction suspends here.
   SELECT ...
   INSERT ...-- Autonomous transaction begins here.
   UPDATE ...
   DELETE ...
   COMMIT;   -- Autonomous transaction ends here.
END;          -- Main transaction resumes here.
```

So, changes made in the main transaction are not visible to the autonomous transaction and if the main transaction holds any locks that the autonomous transaction waits for, a deadlock occurs. Using the NOWAIT option on UPDATE statements in autonomous transactions can help to minimize this kind of deadlock. Functions and procedures (local program, standalone, or packaged), database triggers, top-level anonymous PL/SQL blocks, and object methods can be declared autonomous via the compiler directive PRAGMA AUTONOMOUS_TRANSACTION.

In the example below, the COMMIT does not make permanent pending changes in the calling program. Any rollback in the calling program would also have no effect on the changes committed in this autonomous procedure:

```
CREATE OR REPLACE PROCEDURE add_company (
    name_in    company.name%TYPE
    )
IS
    PRAGMA AUTONOMOUS_TRANSACTION;
BEGIN
    determine_credit(name);
    create_account(name);
    ...
    COMMIT; -- Only commit this procedure's changes.
END add_company;
```

Cursors in PL/SQL

Every SQL statement executed by the RDBMS has a private
SQL area that contains information about the SQL statement and the set of data returned. In PL/SQL, a cursor is a
name assigned to a specific private SQL area for a specific
SQL statement. There can be either static cursors, whose
SQL statement is determined at compile time, or dynamic
cursors, whose SQL statement is determined at runtime.
Static cursors are covered in greater detail in this section.
Dynamic cursors in PL/SQL are implemented via the built-
in package DBMS_SQL. See the book *Oracle Built-in Packages* and the corresponding *Oracle PL/SQL Built-ins Pocket
Reference,* both from O'Reilly & Associates, for full cover-
age on DBMS_SQL and the other built-in packages.

Explicit Cursors

Explicit cursors are SELECT statements that are DECLAREd
explicitly in the declaration section of the current block or
in a package specification. Use OPEN, FETCH, and CLOSE
in the execution or exception sections of your programs.

Declaring explicit cursors

To use an explicit cursor, you must first declare it in the
declaration section of a block or package. There are three
types of explicit cursor declarations:

- A cursor without parameters, such as:

```
CURSOR company_cur
    IS
    SELECT company_id FROM company;
```

- A cursor that accepts arguments through a parameter list:

```
CURSOR company_cur (id_in IN NUMBER) IS
SELECT name FROM company
WHERE  company_id = id_in;
```

- A cursor *header* that contains a RETURN clause in place of the SELECT statement:

```
CURSOR company_cur (id_in IN NUMBER)
RETURN company%ROWTYPE IS
SELECT * FROM company;
```

This technique can be used in packages to hide the implementation of the cursor in the package body. See the "Packages" section for more information.

Opening explicit cursors

To open a cursor, use the following syntax:

```
OPEN cursor_name [(argument [,argument ...])];
```

where *cursor_name* is the name of the cursor as declared in the declaration section. The arguments are required if the definition of the cursor contains a parameter list.

You must open an explicit cursor before you can fetch rows from that cursor. When the cursor is opened, the processing includes the PARSE, BIND, OPEN, and EXECUTE statements. This OPEN processing includes: determining an execution plan, associating host variables and cursor parameters with the placeholders in the SQL statement, determining the result set, and, finally, setting the current row pointer to the first row in the result set.

When using a cursor FOR loop, the OPEN is implicit in the FOR statement. If you try to open a cursor that is already open, PL/SQL will raise an "ORA-06511: PL/SQL: cursor already open" exception.

Fetching from explicit cursors

The FETCH statement places the contents of the current row into local variables. To retrieve all rows in a result set, each row needs to be fetched. The syntax for a FETCH statement is:

```
FETCH cursor_name INTO record_or_variable_list;
```

where *cursor_name* is the name of the cursor as declared and opened.

Closing explicit cursors

The syntax of the CLOSE statement is:

```
CLOSE cursor_name;
```

where *cursor_name* is the name of the cursor declared and opened.

After all rows have been fetched, a cursor needs to be closed. Closing a cursor releases the private SQL area used by the cursor, freeing the memory used by that cursor.

If you declare a cursor in a local anonymous, procedure, or function block, that cursor will automatically close when the block terminates. Package-based cursors must be closed explicitly, or they stay open for the duration of your session. Closing a cursor that is not open raises an INVALID CURSOR exception.

Explicit cursor attributes

There are four attributes associated with cursors: ISOPEN, FOUND, NOTFOUND, and ROWCOUNT. These attributes can be accessed with the % delimiter to obtain information about the state of the cursor. The syntax for a cursor attribute is:

```
cursor_name%attribute
```

where *cursor_name* is the name of the explicit cursor.

The behaviors of the explicit cursor attributes are described in the following table.

Attribute	Description
%ISOPEN	TRUE if cursor is open. FALSE if cursor is not open.
%FOUND	INVALID_CURSOR is raised if cursor has not been OPENed. NULL before the first fetch. TRUE if record was fetched successfully. FALSE if no row was returned. INVALID_CURSOR if cursor has been CLOSEd.
%NOTFOUND	INVALID_CURSOR is raised if cursor has not been OPENed. NULL before the first fetch. FALSE if record was fetched successfully. TRUE if no row was returned. INVALID_CURSOR if cursor has been CLOSEd.
%ROWCOUNT	INVALID_CURSOR is raised if cursor has not been OPENed. The number of rows fetched from the cursor. INVALID_CURSOR if cursor has been CLOSEd.

Frequently a cursor attribute is checked as part of a WHILE loop that fetches rows from a cursor:

```
DECLARE
    caller_rec caller_pkg.caller_cur%ROWTYPE;
BEGIN
    OPEN caller_pkg.caller_cur;
    LOOP
        FETCH caller_pkg.caller_cur into caller_rec;
        EXIT WHEN caller_pkg.caller_cur%NOTFOUND
                  OR
                  caller_pkg.caller_cur%ROWCOUNT > 10;

        UPDATE call
            SET caller_id = caller_rec.caller_id
            WHERE call_timestamp < SYSDATE;
    END LOOP;
    CLOSE caller_pkg.caller_cur;
END;
```

Implicit Cursors

Whenever a SQL statement is directly in the execution or exception section of a PL/SQL block, you are working with implicit cursors. These statements include INSERT, UPDATE, DELETE, and SELECT INTO statements. Unlike explicit cursors, implicit cursors do not need to be declared, OPENed, FETCHed, or CLOSEd.

SELECT statements handle the %FOUND and %NOT-FOUND attributes differently from explicit cursors. When an implicit SELECT statement does not return any rows, PL/SQL immediately raises the NO_DATA_FOUND exception and control passes to the exception section. When an implicit SELECT returns more than one row, PL/SQL immediately raises the TOO_MANY_ROWS exception and control passes to the exception section.

Implicit cursor attributes are referenced via the SQL cursor. For example:

```
BEGIN
    UPDATE activity SET last_accessed := SYSDATE ·
    WHERE UID = user_id;

    IF SQL%NOTFOUND THEN
        INSERT INTO activity_log (uid,last_accessed)
        VALUES (user_id,SYSDATE);
    END IF
END;
```

SQL Attributes	Description
%ISOPEN	Always FALSE since the cursor is opened implicitly and closed immediately after the statement is executed.
%FOUND	NULL before the statement. TRUE if one or more rows were inserted, updated, or deleted or if only one row was selected. FALSE if no row was selected, updated, inserted, or deleted.

SQL Attributes	Description
%NOTFOUND	NULL before the statement. TRUE if no row was selected, updated, inserted, or deleted. FALSE if one or more rows were inserted, updated, or deleted.
%ROWCOUNT	The number of rows affected by the cursor.
%BULK_ROWCOUNT (Oracle8*i*)	A pseudo index-by table containing the numbers of rows affected by the statements executed in bulk bind operations. See the "Bulk Binds (Oracle8*i*)" section for more information on %BULK_ROWCOUNT.

Use the RETURNING clause in INSERT, UPDATE, and DELETE statements to obtain data modified by the associated DML statement. This clause allows you to avoid an additional SELECT statement to query the results of the DML statement. For example:

```
BEGIN
   UPDATE activity SET last_accessed := SYSDATE
   WHERE UID = user_id
   RETURNING last_accessed, cost_center
   INTO timestamp, chargeback_acct;
```

The SELECT FOR UPDATE clause

By default, the Oracle RDBMS locks rows as they are changed. To lock all rows in a result set, use the FOR UPDATE clause in your SELECT statement when you OPEN the cursor, instead of when you change the data. Using the FOR UPDATE clause does not require you to actually make changes to the data; it only locks the rows when opening the cursor. These locks are released on the next COMMIT or ROLLBACK. As always, these row locks do not affect other SELECT statements unless they, too, are FOR UPDATE. The FOR UPDATE clause is appended to the end of the SELECT statement and has the following syntax:

```
SELECT ...
  FROM ...
    FOR UPDATE [OF column_reference] [NOWAIT];
```

where *column_reference* is a comma-delimited list of columns that appear in the SELECT clause. The NOWAIT keyword tells the RDBMS to not wait for other blocking locks to be released. The default is to wait forever.

In the following example, only columns from the inventory (pet) table are referenced FOR UPDATE, so no rows in the *dog_breeds* (dog) table are locked when *hounds_in_stock_cur* is opened:

```
DECLARE
    CURSOR hounds_in_stock_cur IS
        SELECT pet.stock_no, pet.breeder, dog.size
          FROM dog_breeds dog ,inventory pet
         WHERE dog.breed = pet.breed
           AND dog.class = 'HOUND'
           FOR UPDATE OF pet.stock_no, pet.breeder;
BEGIN
```

The WHERE CURRENT OF clause

UPDATE and DELETE statements can use a WHERE CURRENT OF clause if they reference a cursor declared FOR UPDATE. This syntax indicates that the UPDATE or DELETE should modify the current row identified by the FOR UPDATE cursor. The syntax is:

```
[UPDATE | DELETE ] ...
    WHERE CURRENT OF cursor_name;
```

By using WHERE CURRENT OF, you do not have to repeat the WHERE clause in the SELECT statement. For example:

```
DECLARE
    CURSOR wip_cur IS
        SELECT acct_no, enter_date FROM wip
         WHERE enter_date < SYSDATE -7
           FOR UPDATE;
BEGIN
    FOR wip_rec IN wip_cur
    LOOP
        INSERT INTO acct_log (acct_no, order_date)
            VALUES (wip_rec.acct_no, wip_rec.enter_
                date);
```

```
       DELETE FROM wip
           WHERE CURRENT OF wip_cur;
    END LOOP;
  END;
```

Cursor Variables

A cursor variable is a data structure that points to a cursor object, which in turn points to the cursor's result set. You can use cursor variables to more easily retrieve rows in a result set from client and server programs. You can also use cursor variables to hide minor variations in queries.

The syntax for a REF_CURSOR type is:

```
TYPE ref_cursor_name IS REF CURSOR
   [RETURN record_type];
```

If you do not include a RETURN clause, then you are declaring a weak REF CURSOR. Cursor variables declared from weak REF CURSORs can be associated with any query at runtime. A REF CURSOR declaration with a RETURN clause defines a "strong" REF CURSOR. A cursor variable based on a strong REF CURSOR can be associated with queries whose result sets match the number and datatype of the record structure after the RETURN at runtime.

To use cursor variables, you must first create a REF_CURSOR type, then declare a cursor variable based on that type.

The following example shows the use of both weak and strong REF CURSORs:

```
DECLARE
   -- Create a cursor type based on the companies
      table.
   TYPE company_curtype IS REF CURSOR
      RETURN companies%ROWTYPE;

   -- Create the variable based on the REF CURSOR.
   company_cur company_curtype;

   -- And now the weak, general approach.
   TYPE any_curtype IS REF CURSOR;
   generic_curvar any_curtype;
```

The syntax to OPEN a cursor variable is:

```
OPEN cursor_name FOR select_statement;
```

FETCH and CLOSE a cursor variable using the same syntax as for explicit cursors. There are a number of restrictions on cursor variables:

- Cursor variables cannot be declared in a package since they do not have a persistent state.

- You cannot use the FOR UPDATE clause with cursor variables.

- You cannot assign NULLs to a cursor variable nor use comparison operators to test for equality, inequality, or nullity.

- Neither database columns nor collections can store cursor variables.

- You cannot use RPCs to pass cursor variables from one server to another.

- Cursor variables cannot be used with the dynamic SQL built-in package DBMS_SQL.

Exception Handling

PL/SQL allows developers to raise and handle errors (exceptions) in a very flexible and powerful way. Each PL/SQL block can have its own exception section, in which exceptions can be trapped and handled (resolved or passed on to the enclosing block).

When an exception occurs (is raised) in a PL/SQL block, its execution section immediately terminates. Control is passed to the exception section.

Every exception in PL/SQL has an error number and error message; some exceptions also have names.

Declaring Exceptions

Some exceptions (see the following table) have been pre-defined by Oracle in the STANDARD package. You can also declare your own exceptions as follows:

```
DECLARE
    exception_name EXCEPTION;
```

Error	Named Exception
ORA-00001	DUP_VAL_ON_INDEX
ORA-00051	TIMEOUT_ON_RESOURCE
ORA-01001	INVALID_CURSOR
ORA-01012	NOT_LOGGED_ON
ORA-01017	LOGIN_DENIED
ORA-01403	NO_DATA_FOUND
ORA-01410	SYS_INVALID_ROWID
ORA-01422	TOO_MANY_ROWS
ORA-01476	ZERO_DIVIDE
ORA-01722	INVALID_NUMBER
ORA-06500	STORAGE_ERROR
ORA-06501	PROGRAM_ERROR
ORA-06502	VALUE_ERROR
ORA-06504	ROWTYPE_MISMATCH
ORA-06511	CURSOR_ALREADY_OPEN
ORA-06530	ACCESS_INTO_NULL
ORA-06531	COLLECTION_IS_NULL
ORA-06532	SUBSCRIPT_OUTSIDE_LIMIT
ORA-06533	SUBSCRIPT_BEYOND_COUNT

An exception can be declared only once in a block, but nested blocks can declare an exception with the same name as an outer block. If this multiple declaration occurs, scope takes precedence over name when handling the exception. The inner block's declaration takes precedence over a global declaration.

When you declare your own exception, you must RAISE it explicitly. All declared exceptions have an error code of 1 and the error message "User-defined exception," unless you use the EXCEPTION_INIT pragma.

You can associate an error number with a declared exception with the PRAGMA EXCEPTION_INIT statement:

```
DECLARE
    exception_name EXCEPTION;
    PRAGMA EXCEPTION_INIT (exception_name,
        error_number);
```

where *error_number* is a literal value (variable references are not allowed). This number can be an Oracle error, such as −1855, or an error in the user-definable −20000 to −20999 range.

Raising Exceptions

An exception can be raised in three ways:

- By the PL/SQL runtime engine
- By an explicit RAISE statement in your code
- By a call to the built-in function RAISE_APPLICATION_ ERROR

The syntax for the RAISE statement is:

```
RAISE exception_name;
```

where *exception_name* is the name of an exception that you have declared, or that is declared in the STANDARD package.

If you use the RAISE statement inside an exception handler, you can leave off an exception name to re-raise the current exception:

```
RAISE;
```

This syntax is not valid outside the exception section.

The RAISE_APPLICATION_ERROR built-in has the following header:

```
RAISE_APPLICATION_ERROR (
    num BINARY_INTEGER,
    msg VARCHAR2,
    keeperrorstack BOOLEAN DEFAULT FALSE);
```

where *num* is the error number (an integer between
–20999 and –20000), *msg* is the associated error message,
and *keeperrorstack* controls the contents of the error stack.

Scope

The scope of an exception section is that portion of the
code that is "covered" by the exception section. An exception handler will only handle or attempt to handle
exceptions raised in the executable section of the PL/SQL
block. Exceptions raised in the declaration or exception
sections are automatically passed to the outer block. Any
line or set of PL/SQL code can be placed inside its own
block and given its own exception section. This allows you
to limit the propagation of an exception.

Propagation

Exceptions raised in a PL/SQL block propagate to an outer
block if they are unhandled or re-raised in the exception
section. When an exception occurs, PL/SQL looks for an
exception handler that checks for the exception (or is the
WHEN OTHERS clause) in the current block. If a match is
not found, then PL/SQL propagates the exception to the
enclosing block or calling program. This propagation con-
tinues until the exception is handled or propagated out of
the outermost block, back to the calling program. In this
case, the exception is "unhandled" and (1) stops the calling program, and (2) causes an automatic rollback of any
outstanding transactions.

Once an exception is handled, it will not propagate
upward. If you want to trap an exception, display a mean-
ingful error message, and have the exception propagate
upward as an error, you must re-raise the exception. The

RAISE statement can re-raise the current exception or raise
a new exception:

```
PROCEDURE delete_dept(deptno_in IN NUMBER)
DECLARE
    still_have_employees EXCEPTION
    PRAGMA EXCEPTION_INIT(still_have_employees.
       -2292)
BEGIN
DELETE FROM dept
WHERE deptno = deptno_in;
EXCEPTION
    WHEN still_have_employees
    THEN
        DBMS_OUTPUT.PUT_LINE
('Please delete employees in dept first');
ROLLBACK;
RAISE;  /* Re-raise the current exception. */
END;
```

The WHEN OTHERS clause

```
EXCEPTION
    WHEN OTHERS
    THEN
        ...
```

Use the WHEN OTHERS clause in the exception handler as
a catch-all to trap any exceptions that are not handled by
specific WHEN clauses in the exception section. If present,
this clause must be the last exception handler in the exception section.

SQLCODE and SQLERRM

SQLCODE and SQLERRM are built-in functions that provide the SQL error code and message for the current
exception. Use these functions inside the exception section's WHEN OTHERS clause to handle specific errors by
number. The EXCEPTION_INIT pragma allows you to handle errors by name.

```
CREATE TABLE err_test
   (widget_name    VARCHAR2(100)
   ,widget_count   NUMBER
   ,CONSTRAINT no_small_numbers CHECK
      (widget_count > 1000));
```

```
BEGIN
   INSERT INTO err_test (widget_name, widget_count)
   VALUES ('Athena',2);
EXCEPTION
   WHEN OTHERS THEN
   IF SQLCODE = -2290
      AND SQLERRM LIKE '%NO_SMALL_NUMBERS%'
   THEN
      DBMS_OUTPUT.PUT_LINE('widget_count is too
         small');
   ELSE
      DBMS_OUTPUT.PUT_LINE('Exception not hooked,'
         ||'SQLcode='||SQLCODE);
      DBMS_OUTPUT.PUT_LINE(SQLERRM);
   END IF;
END;
```

Gives the output of:

```
widget_count is too small
```

The DBMS_UTILITY.FORMAT_ERROR_STACK and DBMS_
UTILITY.FORMAT_CALL_STACK procedures can be used to
capture the full error stack and call stack. See the O'Reilly
& Associates book *Oracle PL/SQL Built-in Packages* for
more information on DBMS_UTILITY.

Exceptions and DML

When an exception is raised in a PL/SQL block, it does *not*
rollback your current transaction, even if the block itself
issued an INSERT, UPDATE, or DELETE. You must issue
your own ROLLBACK statement if you want to clean up
your transaction due to the exception.

If your exception goes unhandled (propagates out of the
outermost block), however, most host environments will
then force an automatic, unqualified rollback of any outstanding changes in your session.

Records in PL/SQL

A PL/SQL record is a data structure composed of multiple
pieces of information called *fields*. To use a record, you
must first define it and declare a variable of this type.

There are three types of records: table-based, cursor-based, and programmer-defined.

Declaring Records

You define and declare records either in the declaration section of a PL/SQL block, or globally, via a package specification.

You do not have to explicitly define table-based or cursor-based records, as they are implicitly defined with the same structure as a table or cursor. Variables of these types are declared via the %ROWTYPE attribute. The record's fields correspond to the table's columns or the columns in the SELECT list. For example:

```
DECLARE
    -- Declare table-based record for company table.
    comp_rec    company%ROWTYPE

    CURSOR comp_summary_cur IS
        SELECT C.company_id,SUM(S.gross_sales) gross
          FROM company C ,sales S
         WHERE C.company_id = S.company_id;

    -- Declare a cursor-based record.
    comp_summary_rec comp_summary_cur%ROWTYPE;
```

Programmer-defined records must be explicitly defined in the PL/SQL block or a package specification with the TYPE statement. Variables of this type can then be declared:

```
DECLARE
    TYPE name_rectype IS RECORD(
        prefix        VARCHAR2(15)
        ,first_name   VARCHAR2(30)
        ,middle_name  VARCHAR2(30)
        ,sur_name     VARCHAR2(30)
        ,suffix       VARCHAR2(10) );

    TYPE employee_rectype IS RECORD (
        emp_id        NUMBER(10) NOT NULL
        ,mgr_id       NUMBER(10)
        ,dept_no      dept.deptno%TYPE
        ,title        VARCHAR2(20)
        ,name         empname_rectype
```

```
      ,hire_date    DATE := SYSDATE
      ,fresh_out    BOOLEAN );

  -- Declare a variable of this type.
  new_emp_rec employee_rectype;
BEGIN
```

Referencing Fields of Records

Individual fields are referenced via dot notation:

```
record_name.field_name
```

For example:

```
employee.first_name
```

Individual fields within a record can be read from or written to. They can appear on either the left or right side of the assignment operator:

```
BEGIN
   insurance_start_date := new_emp_rec.hire_date +
      30;
   new_emp_rec.fresh_out := FALSE;
   ...
```

Record Assignment

An entire record can be assigned to another record of the same type, but one record cannot be compared to another record via Boolean operators. This is a valid assignment:

```
shipto_address_rec := customer_address_rec
```

This is not a valid comparison:

```
IF shipto_address_rec = customer_address_rec
THEN
   ...
END IF;
```

The individual fields of the records need to be compared instead.

Values can be assigned to records or to the fields within a record in four different ways:

- The assignment operator can be used to assign a value to a field:

```
new_emp_rec.hire_date := SYSDATE;
```

- You can SELECT INTO a whole record or the individual fields:

```
SELECT emp_id,dept,title,hire_date,college_recruit
  INTO new_emp_rec
  FROM emp
 WHERE surname = 'LI'
```

- You can FETCH INTO a whole record or the individual fields:

```
FETCH emp_cur INTO new_emp_rec;
FETCH emp_cur INTO new_emp_rec.emp_id,
   new_emp_rec.name;
```

- You can assign all of the fields of one record variable to another record variable of the same type:

```
IF rehire THEN
  new_emp_rec := former_emp_rec;
ENDIF;
```

This aggregate assignment technique works only for records declared with the same TYPE statement.

Nested Records

Nested records are records contained in fields that are records themselves. Nesting records is a powerful way to normalize data structures and hide complexity within PL/SQL programs. For example:

```
DECLARE
   -- Define a record.
   TYPE phone_rectype IS RECORD (
       area_code  VARCHAR2(3),
       exchange   VARCHAR2(3),
       phn_number VARCHAR2(4),
       extension  VARCHAR2(4));

   -- Define a record composed of records.
   TYPE contact_rectype IS RECORD (
       day_phone#  phone_rectype,
       eve_phone#  phone_rectype,
       cell_phone# phone_rectype);
```

```
-- Declare a variable for the nested record.
   auth_rep_info_rec contact_rectype;
BEGIN
```

Named Program Units

The PL/SQL programming language allows you to create a variety of named program units (containers for code). They include:

Procedure
   A program that executes one or more statements

Function
   A program that returns a value

Package
   A container for procedures, functions, and data structures

Triggers
   Programs that execute in response to database changes

Object type
   Oracle8's version of a SQL3 named row type; object types can contain member procedures and functions

Procedures

Procedures are program units that execute one or more statements and can receive or return zero or more values through their parameter lists. The syntax of a procedure is:

```
CREATE [OR REPLACE] PROCEDURE name
   [ (parameter [,parameter]) ]
   [AUTHID  CURRENT_USER | DEFINER ] -- Oracle8i
   [DETERMINISTIC]                    -- Oracle8i
IS | AS
   declaration_section
BEGIN
   executable_section
[EXCEPTION
   exception_section]
END [name];
```

A procedure is called as a standalone executable PL/SQL statement:

```
apply_discount(new_company_id, 0.15) --15% discount
```

Functions

Functions are program units that execute one or more statements and return a value through the RETURN clause. Functions can also receive or return zero or more values through their parameter lists. The syntax of a function is:

```
CREATE [OR REPLACE] FUNCTION name
   [ (parameter [,parameter]) ]
   RETURN return_datatype
   [AUTHID  CURRENT_USER | DEFINER ] -- Oracle8i
   [DETERMINISTIC]                   -- Oracle8i
   [PARALLEL_ENABLE]                 -- Oracle8i
IS | AS
   [declaration_section]
BEGIN
   executable_section
[EXCEPTION
   exception_section]
END [name];
```

A function must have at least one RETURN statement in the execution section. The RETURN clause in the function header specifies the datatype of the returned value.

See the "Compiling stored PL/SQL programs" section for information on the key words OR REPLACE, AUTHID, DETERMINISTIC, and PARALLEL_ENABLE.

See the "Privileges and stored PL/SQL" section for additional information on the key word AUTHID.

A function can be called anywhere an expression of the same type can be used. You can call a function:

* In an assignment statement:

```
sales95 := tot_sales(1995,'C');
```

* To set a default value:

```
DECLARE
   sales95 NUMBER DEFAULT tot_sales(1995,'C');
BEGIN
```

- In a Boolean expression:

```
IF tot_sales(1995,'C') > 10000
THEN
  ...
```

- In a SQL statement:

```
SELECT first_name ,surname
  FROM sellers
WHERE tot_sales(1995,'C') > 1000;
```

- As an argument in another program unit's parameter list.

Here, for example, *max_discount* is a programmer-defined function and SYSDATE is a built-in function:

```
apply_discount(company_id, max_discount(SYSDATE));
```

Parameters

Procedures, functions, and cursors may have a parameter list. This list contains one or more parameters that allow you to pass information back and forth between the subprogram and the calling program. Each parameter is defined by its name, datatype, mode, and optional default value. The syntax for a parameter is:

```
parameter_name [mode] [NOCOPY] datatype
  [(:= | DEFAULT) value]
```

Datatype

The datatype can be any PL/SQL or programmer-defined datatype, but cannot be constrained by a size (NUMBER is valid, NUMBER(10) is not valid). The actual size of the parameter is determined from the calling program or via a %TYPE constraint.

```
CREATE OR REPLACE PROCEDURE empid_to_name
(in_id           emp.emp_id%TYPE -- Compiles OK.
,out_last_name   VARCHAR2        -- Compiles OK.
,out_first_name  VARCHAR2(10)    -- Won't compile.
) IS
  ...
```

The lengths of *out_last_name* and *out_first_name* are determined by the calling program:

```
DECLARE
   surname       VARCHAR2(10);
   first_name    VARCHAR2(10);
BEGIN
   empid_to_name(10, surname, first_name);
END;
```

Mode

The mode of a parameter specifies whether the parameter can be read from or written to, as shown in the following table.

Mode	Description	Parameter Usage
IN	Read-only	The value of the actual parameter can be referenced inside the program, but the parameter cannot be changed.
OUT	Write-only	The program can assign a value to the parameter, but the parameter's value cannot be referenced.
IN OUT	Read/write	The program can both reference (read) and modify (write) the parameter.

If the mode is not explicitly defined, it defaults to IN.

OUT parameters can be written to. In Oracle7, OUT parameters can appear only on the left side of an assignment operation. In Oracle8 and above, OUT parameters are read/write and hence can appear on either side of an assignment. If an exception is raised during execution of a procedure or function, assignments made to OUT or IN OUT parameters get rolled back.

The NOCOPY (Oracle8*i*) compiler hint for parameters makes the parameter a call by reference instead of a call by value. Normally, PL/SQL passes IN/OUT parameters by value—a copy of the parameter is created for the subprogram. When parameter items get large, like collections or objects, the copy can eat memory and slow the processing. NOCOPY directs PL/SQL to pass the parameter by reference, using a pointer to the single copy of the parameter. The disadvantage of NOCOPY is that when an exception is raised during execution of a program that has modified an OUT or IN OUT parameter, the changes to the actual parameters are not rolled back because the parameters were passed by reference instead of being copied.

Default values

IN parameters can be given default values. If an IN parameter has a default value, then you do not need to supply an argument for that parameter when you call the program unit. It automatically uses the default value. For example:

```
CREATE OR REPLACE PROCEDURE hire_employee
(emp_id      IN VARCHAR2
,hire_date   IN DATE := SYSDATE
,company_id  IN NUMBER := 1
) IS
...

-- Example calls to the procedure.
-- Use two default values.
hire_employee(new_empno);
-- Use one default value.
hire_employee(new_empno,'12-Jan-1999');
-- Use non-trailing default value, named notation.
hire_employee(emp_id=>new_empno, comp_id=>12);
```

Parameter-passing notations

Formal parameters are the names that are declared in the header of a procedure or function. *Actual parameters* are the values or expressions placed in the parameter list when a procedure or function is called. In the *empid_to_name* example shown earlier in the "Datatype" section, the actual parameters to the procedure are *in_id*, *out_last_name*, and *out_first_name*. The formal parameters used in the call to this procedure are 10, *surname*, and *first_name*.

PL/SQL lets you use either of two styles for passing arguments in parameter lists: positional or named notation.

Positional notation

This is the default. Each value in the list of arguments supplied in the program call is associated with the parameter in the corresponding position.

Named notation

This explicitly associates the argument value with its parameter by name (not position). When you use named notation, you can supply the arguments in any order and you can skip over IN arguments that have default values.

The call to the *empid_to_name* procedure is shown here with both notations:

```
BEGIN
    -- Implicit positional notation.
    empid_to_name(10, surname, first_name);

    -- Explicit named notation.
    empid_to_name(in_id=>10
        ,out_last_name=>surname
        ,out_first_name=>first_name);
END;
```

When calling stored functions from SQL, named notation is not supported.

Local program

A local program is a procedure or function that is defined in the declaration section of a PL/SQL block. The declaration of a local program must appear at the end of the declaration section, after the declarations of any types, records, cursors, variables, and exceptions. A program defined in a declaration section may only be referenced within that block's executable and exception sections. It is not defined outside that block.

The following program defines a local procedure and function:

```
PROCEDURE track_revenue
IS
    PROCEDURE calc_total (year_in IN INTEGER) IS
```

```
BEGIN
   calculations here ...
END;

FUNCTION below_minimum (comp_id IN INTEGER)
   RETURN BOOLEAN
IS
BEGIN
   ...
END;
```

Local programs may be overloaded with the same restrictions as overloaded packaged programs.

Program overloading

PL/SQL allows you to define two or more programs with the same name within any declaration section, including a package specification or body. This is called *overloading*. If two or more programs have the same name, they must be different in some other way so that the compiler can determine which program should be used.

Here is an example of overloaded programs in a built-in package specification:

```
PACKAGE DBMS_OUTPUT
IS
   PROCEDURE PUT_LINE (a VARCHAR2);
   PROCEDURE PUT_LINE (a NUMBER);
   PROCEDURE PUT_LINE (a DATE);
END;
```

Each PUT_LINE procedure is identical, except for the datatype of the parameter. That is enough difference for the compiler.

To overload programs successfully, one or more of the following conditions must be true:

- Parameters must differ by datatype family (number, character, datetime, or Boolean).

- The program type must be different (you can overload a function and a procedure of the same name and identical parameter list).

- The numbers of parameters must be different.

You *cannot* overload programs if:

- Only the datatypes of the functions' RETURN clauses are different.

- Parameter datatypes are within the same family (CHAR and VARCHAR2, NUMBER and INTEGER, etc.).

- Only the modes of the parameters are different.

Forward declarations

Programs must be declared before they can be used. PL/SQL supports *mutual recursion*, in which program A calls program B, whereupon program B calls program A. To implement this mutual recursion, you must use a *forward declaration* of the programs. This technique declares a program in advance of the program definition, thus making it available for other programs to use. The forward declaration is the program header up to the IS/AS keyword:

```
PROCEDURE perform_calc(year_in IN NUMBER)
IS
   /* Forward declaration for total_cost
      function. */
   FUNCTION total_cost (...) RETURN NUMBER;

   /* The net_profit function can now use
      total_cost. */
   FUNCTION net_profit(...) RETURN NUMBER
   IS
   BEGIN
      RETURN total_sales(...) - total_cost(...);
   END;

   /* The Total_cost function calls net_profit. */
   FUNCTION total_cost (...) RETURN NUMBER
   IS
   BEGIN
      IF net_profit(...) < 0
      THEN
         RETURN 0;
         ELSE
         RETURN...;
      END IF;
   END;
```

```
BEGIN /* procedure perform_calc */
   ...
END perform_calc;
```

Compiling stored PL/SQL programs

The following keywords are new with Oracle8*i*:

OR REPLACE
Used to rebuild an existing program unit, preserving its privileges.

AUTHID
Defines whether the program will execute with the privileges of, and resolve names like, the object owner (DEFINER), or as the user executing the function (CURRENT_USER). Prior to Oracle8*i,* only the built-in packages DBMS_SQL and DBMS_UTILITY executed as CURRENT_USER. The default AUTHID is DEFINER.

REPEATABLE
Required for functions and any dependent programs used in domain (application-defined) indexes.

DETERMINISTIC
Required for function-based indexes. A function is DETERMINISTIC if it does not meaningfully reference package variables or the database.

PARALLEL_ENABLED
Tells the optimizer that a function is safe for parallel execution. It replaces the statement:

```
PRAGMA RESTRICT REFERENCES (function_name, wnps,
   rnps, wnds, rnds);
```

Privileges and stored PL/SQL

Unless you're using an invoker's rights program in Oracle8*i,* roles cannot provide object or system privileges that can be used inside stored PL/SQL. You must have privileges granted directly to you for objects that, rather than owning, you reference in stored SQL or PL/SQL (procedures, functions, packages, triggers, and views). This restriction arises from the manner in which the database obtains privileges and checks for objects referenced from SQL.

Direct GRANT and REVOKE privileges cannot be different for two concurrent sessions of the same user, while roles can be disabled in only one session. Privileges are checked when stored PL/SQL is compiled, and since only GRANT and REVOKE privileges can be relied upon to remain enabled, they are the only privileges checked.

This direct GRANT restriction does not apply for anonymous PL/SQL blocks because such blocks are compiled at runtime when all privileges are known. It also does not apply for procedures and functions with the AUTHID of CURRENT_USER (Oracle8*i*).

Triggers

Triggers are programs that execute in response to changes in table data or certain database events. There is a predefined set of events that can be "hooked" with a trigger, enabling you to integrate your own processing with that of the database. A triggering event *fires* or executes the trigger.

Creating Triggers

The syntax for creating a trigger is:

```
CREATE [OR REPLACE] TRIGGER trigger_name
BEFORE | AFTER | INSTEAD OF trigger_event
   ON
   [ NESTED TABLE nested_table_column OF view ]
      | table_or_view_reference | DATABASE
   [referencing_clause]
[FOR EACH ROW [WHEN trigger_condition]]
trigger_body;
```

INSTEAD OF triggers are valid on only Oracle8 views. Oracle8*i* must create a trigger on a nested table column.

Trigger events are defined in the following table.

Trigger Event	Description
INSERT	Fires whenever a row is added to the *table_reference*.
UPDATE	Fires whenever an UPDATE changes the *table_reference*. UPDATE triggers can additionally specify an OF clause to restrict firing to updates OF certain columns. See the following examples.
DELETE	Fires whenever a row is deleted from the *table_reference*. Does not fire on TRUN-CATE of the table.
CREATE (Oracle8*i*)	Fires whenever a CREATE statement adds a new object to the database. In this context, objects are things like tables or packages (found in ALL_OBJECTS). Can apply to single schema or the entire database.
ALTER (Oracle8*i*)	Fires whenever an ALTER statement changes a database object. In this context, objects are things like tables or packages (found in ALL_OBJECTS). Can apply to single schema or the entire database.
DROP (Oracle8*i*)	Fires whenever a DROP statement removes an object from the database. In this context, objects are things like tables or packages (found in ALL_OBJECTS). Can apply to a single schema or the entire database.
SERVERERROR (Oracle8*i*)	Fires whenever a server error message is logged. Only AFTER triggers are allowed in this context.
LOGON (Oracle8*i*)	Fires whenever a session is created (a user connects to the database). Only AFTER triggers are allowed in this context.
LOGOFF (Oracle8*i*)	Fires whenever a session is terminated (a user disconnects from the database). Only BEFORE triggers are allowed in this context.
STARTUP (Oracle8*i*)	Fires when the database is opened. Only AFTER triggers are allowed in this context.
SHUTDOWN (Oracle8*i*)	Fires when the database is closed. Only BEFORE triggers are allowed in this context.

Triggers can fire BEFORE or AFTER the triggering event. AFTER data triggers are slightly more efficient than BEFORE triggers.

The *referencing_clause* is only allowed for the data events INSERT, UPDATE, and DELETE. It lets you give a non-default name to the old and new pseudo-records. These pseudo-records give the program visibility to the pre- and post-change values in row-level triggers. These records are defined like %ROWTYPE records, except that columns of type LONG or LONG RAW cannot be referenced. They are prefixed with a colon in the trigger body, and referenced with dot notation. Unlike other records, these fields can only be assigned individually—aggregate assignment is not allowed. All old fields are NULL within INSERT triggers, and all new fields are NULL within DELETE triggers.

FOR EACH ROW defines the trigger to be a row-level trigger. Row-level triggers fire once for each row affected. The default is a statement-level trigger, which fires only once for each triggering statement.

The WHEN *trigger_condition* specifies the conditions that must be met for the trigger to fire. Stored functions and object methods are not allowed in the trigger condition.

The trigger body is a standard PL/SQL block. For example:

```
CREATE OR REPLACE TRIGGER add_uid
   BEFORE INSERT ON emp
   REFERENCING NEW as new_row
   FOR EACH ROW
   BEGIN
      -- Automatically timestamp the entry.
      SELECT SYSDATE INTO :new_row.entry_date
         FROM dual;
END add_uid;
```

Triggers are enabled on creation, and can be disabled (so they do not fire) with an ALTER statement:

```
ALTER TRIGGER trigger_name ENABLE | DISABLE;

ALTER TABLE table_name ENABLE | DISABLE ALL
   TRIGGERS;
```

Trigger Predicates

When using a single trigger for multiple events, use the trigger predicates INSERTING, UPDATING, and DELETING in the trigger condition to identify the triggering event:

```
CREATE OR REPLACE TRIGGER emp_log_t
   AFTER INSERT OR UPDATE OR DELETE ON emp
   FOR EACH ROW
DECLARE
   dmltype  CHAR(1);
BEGIN
   IF INSERTING THEN
       dmltype := 'I';
       INSERT INTO emp_log (emp_no, who, operation)
          VALUES (:new.empno, USER, dmltype);
   ELSIF UPDATING THEN
       dmltype := 'U';
       INSERT INTO emp_log (emp_no, who, operation)
          VALUES (:new.empno, USER, dmltype);
   END IF;
END;
```

DML Events

The DML events include INSERT, UPDATE, or DELETE statements on a table or view. Triggers on these events can be statement- (table only) or row-level triggers and can fire BEFORE or AFTER the triggering event. BEFORE triggers can modify the data in affected rows, but perform an additional logical read. AFTER triggers do not perform this additional logical read, and therefore perform slightly better, but are not able to change the *:new* values. Triggers cannot be created on SYS-owned objects. The order in which these triggers fire, if present, is as follows:

1. BEFORE statement-level trigger

2. For each row affected by the statement:

   a. BEFORE row-level trigger

   b. The triggering statement

   c. AFTER row-level trigger

3. AFTER statement-level trigger

DDL Events (Oracle8i)

The DDL events are CREATE, ALTER, and DROP. These triggers fire whenever the respective DDL statement is executed. DDL triggers can apply to either a single schema or the entire database.

Database Events (Oracle8i)

The database events are SERVERERROR, LOGON, LOGOFF, STARTUP, and SHUTDOWN. Only BEFORE triggers are allowed for LOGOFF and SHUTDOWN events. Only AFTER triggers are allowed for LOGON, STARTUP, and SERVERERROR events. A SHUTDOWN trigger will fire on a SHUTDOWN NORMAL and a SHUTDOWN IMMEDIATE, but not on a SHUTDOWN ABORT.

Packages

A *package* is a collection of PL/SQL objects that are grouped together.

There are a number of benefits to using packages, including information hiding, object-oriented design, top-down design, object persistence across transactions, and improved performance.

Elements that can be placed in a package include procedures, functions, constants, variables, cursors, exception names, and TYPE statements (for index-by tables, records, REF CURSORs, etc.).

Overview of Package Structure

A package can have two parts: the specification and the body. The *package specification* is required and lists all the objects that are publicly available (may be referenced from outside the package) for use in applications. It also provides all the information a developer needs in order to use objects in the package; essentially, it is the package's API.

The *package body* contains all code needed to implement procedures, functions, and cursors listed in the specification, as well as any private objects (accessible only to other elements defined in that package), and an optional initialization section.

If a package specification does not contain any procedures or functions and no private code is needed, then that package does not need to have a package body.

The syntax for the package specification is:

```
CREATE [OR REPLACE] PACKAGE package_name
[ AUTHID CURRENT_USER | DEFINER ]    -- Oracle8i
IS | AS

   [definitions of public TYPEs
   ,declarations of public variables, types and
      objects
   ,declarations of exceptions
   ,pragmas
   ,declarations of cursors, procedures and
      functions
   ,headers of procedures and functions]

END [package_name];
```

The syntax for the package body is:

```
CREATE [OR REPLACE] PACKAGE BODY package_name
   IS | AS

   [definitions of private TYPEs
   ,declarations of private variables, types and
      objects
   ,full definitions of cursors
   ,full definitions of procedures and functions]

[BEGIN
   executable_statements

[EXCEPTION
   exception_handlers ] ]

END [package_name];
```

The optional **OR REPLACE** keywords are used to rebuild an existing package, preserving its privileges. The declarations in the specifications cannot be repeated in the body. Both

---

the executable section and the exception section are optional in a package body. If the executable section is present, it is called the *initialization section* and executes only once—the first time any package element is referenced during a session.

You must compile the package specification before the body specification. When you grant EXECUTE authority on a package to another schema or to PUBLIC, you are giving access only to the specification; the body remains hidden.

Here's an example of a package:

```
CREATE OR REPLACE PACKAGE time_pkg IS
    FUNCTION GetTimestamp RETURN DATE;
    PRAGMA RESTRICT_REFERENCES (GetTimestamp, WNDS);

    PROCEDURE ResetTimestamp;
END time_pkg;

CREATE OR REPLACE PACKAGE BODY time_pkg IS
    StartTimeStamp    DATE := SYSDATE;
    -- StartTimeStamp is package data.

    FUNCTION GetTimestamp RETURN DATE IS
    BEGIN
        RETURN StartTimeStamp;
    END GetTimestamp;

    PROCEDURE ResetTimestamp IS
    BEGIN
        StartTimeStamp := SYSDATE;
    END ResetTimestamp;

END time_pkg;
```

Referencing Package Elements

The elements declared in the specification are referenced from the calling application via dot notation:

```
package_name.package_element
```

For example, the built-in package DBMS_OUTPUT has a procedure PUT_LINE, so a call to this package would look like this:

```
DBMS_OUTPUT.PUT_LINE('This is parameter data');
```

Package Data

Data structures declared within a package specification or body, but outside any procedure or function in the package, are *package data*. The scope of package data is your entire session; it spans transaction boundaries, acting as globals for your programs.

Keep the following guidelines in mind as you work with package data:

- The state of your package variables is not affected by COMMITs and ROLLBACKs.

- A cursor declared in a package has global scope. It remains OPEN until you close it explicitly or your session ends.

- A good practice is to *hide* your data structures in the package body and provide "get and set" programs to read and write that data. This technique protects your data.

The SERIALLY_REUSABLE pragma

If you need package data to exist only during a call to the packaged functions or procedures, and not between calls of the current session, you can save runtime memory by using the pragma SERIALLY_REUSABLE. After each call, PL/SQL closes the cursors and releases the memory used in the package. This technique is applicable only to large user communities executing the same routine. Normally, the database server's memory requirements grow linearly with the number of users; with SERIALLY_REUSABLE, this growth can be less than linear, since work areas for package states are kept in a pool in the SGA (System Global Area) and are shared among all users. This pragma must appear in both the specification and the body:

```
CREATE OR REPLACE PACKAGE my_pkg IS
   PRAGMA SERIALLY_REUSABLE;
   PROCEDURE foo;
```

```
END my_pkg;

CREATE OR REPLACE PACKAGE BODY my_pkg IS
    PRAGMA SERIALLY_REUSABLE;
    PROCEDURE foo IS
    ...
END my_pkg;
```

Package Initialization

The first time a user references a package element, the
entire package is loaded into the SGA of the database
instance to which the user is connected. That code is then
shared by all sessions that have EXECUTE authority on the
package.

Any package data are then instantiated into the session's
UGA (User Global Area), a private area in either the SGA or
PGA (Program Global Area). If the package body contains
an initialization section, that code will be executed. The initialization section is optional and appears at the end of the
package body, beginning with a BEGIN statement and end-
ing with the EXCEPTION section (if present) or the END of
the package.

The following package initialization section runs a query to
transfer the user's minimum balance into a global package
variable. Programs can then reference the packaged variable (via the function) to retrieve the balance, rather than
executing the query repeatedly:

```
CREATE OR REPLACE PACKAGE usrinfo
IS
    FUNCTION minbal RETURN VARCHAR2;
END usrinfo;
/

CREATE OR REPLACE PACKAGE BODY usrinfo
IS
    g_minbal NUMBER; -- Package data
    FUNCTION minbal RETURN VARCHAR2
        IS BEGIN RETURN g_minbal; END;
BEGIN   -- Initialization section
    SELECT minimum_balance
```

```
      INTO g_minbal
      FROM user_configuration
      WHERE username = USER;
EXCEPTION
   WHEN NO_DATA_FOUND
   THEN g_minbal := NULL;
END usrinfo;
```

Calling PL/SQL Functions in SQL

Stored functions can be called from SQL statements in a
manner similar to built-in functions like DECODE, NVL, or
RTRIM. This is a powerful technique for incorporating busi-
ness rules into SQL in a simple and elegant way.
Unfortunately, there are a number of caveats and
restrictions.

The most notable caveat is that stored functions executed
from SQL are not guaranteed to follow the read consistency model of the database. Unless the SQL statement and
any stored functions in that statement are in the same read-
consistent transaction (even if they are read-only), each
execution of the stored function will look at a different
time-consistent set of data. To avoid this potential prob-
lem, you need to ensure read consistency programmatically
by issuing the SET TRANSACTION READ ONLY or SET
TRANSACTION SERIALIZABLE statement before executing
your SQL statement containing the stored function. A COM-
MIT or ROLLBACK then needs to follow the SQL statement
to end this read-consistent transaction.

Syntax for Calling Stored Functions
in SQL

The syntax for calling a stored function from SQL is the
same as referencing it from PL/SQL:

```
[schema_name.][pkg_name.]func_name[@db_link]
   [parm_list]
```

schema_name is optional and refers to the user/owner of the function or package. *pkg_name* is optional and refers to the package containing the called function. *func_name* is mandatory and is the function name. *db_link* is optional and refers to the database link name to the remote database containing the function. *parm_list* is optional, as are the parameters passed to the function.

The following are example calls to the GetTimestamp function in the *time_pkg* example seen earlier in the "Overview of Package Structure" section:

```
-- Capture system events.
INSERT INTO v_sys_event (timestamp ,event
   ,qty_waits)
   SELECT time_pkg.GetTimestamp ,event ,total_waits
   FROM v$system_event

-- Capture system statistics.
INSERT INTO v_sys_stat (timestamp,stat#,value)
   SELECT time_pkg.GetTimestamp ,statistic# ,value
   FROM v$sysstat;
```

Requirements and Restrictions on Stored Functions in SQL

There are a number of requirements for calling stored functions in SQL:

- The function must be a single-row function—not one that operates on a column or group function.

- All parameters must be IN; no IN OUT or OUT parameters are allowed.

- The datatypes of the function's parameters and RETURN must be compatible with RDBMS datatypes. You cannot have arguments or RETURN types like BOOLEAN, programmer-defined record, index-by table, etc.

- The parameters passed to the function must use positional notation; named notation is not supported.

- Functions defined in packages must have a RESTRICT_
  REFERENCES pragma in the specification (Oracle8.0 and
  earlier).

- The function must be stored in the database, not a local
  program, Developer/2000 PL/SQL library, or Form.

Calling Packaged Functions in SQL

Prior to Oracle8*i* Release 8.1, it was necessary to assert the
purity level of a packaged procedure or function when using
it directly or indirectly in a SQL statement. Beginning with
Oracle8*i* Release 8.1, the PL/SQL runtime engine determines
a program's purity level automatically if no assertion exists.

The RESTRICT_REFERENCES pragma asserts a purity level.
The syntax for the RESTRICT_REFERENCES pragma is:

```
PRAGMA RESTRICT_REFERENCES (program_name |
    DEFAULT, purity_level);
```

The keyword DEFAULT applies to all methods of an object
type or all programs in a package.

There can be from one to five purity levels, in any order, in
a comma-delimited list. The purity level describes to what
extent the program or method is free of *side effects*. Side
effects are listed in the following table with the purity levels they address.

Purity Level	Description	Restriction
WNDS	Write No Data-base State	Executes no INSERT, UPDATE, or DELETE statements.
RNDS	Read No Data-base State	Executes no SELECT state-ments.
WNPS	Write No Package State	Does not modify any package variables.
RNPS	Read No Package State	Does not read any package variables.
TRUST (Oracle8*i*)		Does not enforce the restrictions declared but allows the compiler to trust they are true.

The purity level requirements for packaged functions are different depending on where in the SQL statement the stored functions are used:

- To be called from SQL, all stored functions must assert WNDS.

- All functions not used in a SELECT, VALUES, or SET clause must assert WNPS.

- To be executed remotely, the function must assert WNPS and RNPS.

- To be executed in parallel, the function must assert all four purity levels or, in Oracle8*i*, use PARALLEL_ENABLED in the declaration.

- These functions must not call any other program that does not also assert the minimum purity level.

- If a package has an initialization section, it too must assert purity in Oracle7.

- If a function is overloaded, each overloading must assert its own purity level, and the levels don't have to be the same. To do this, place the pragma immediately after each overloaded declaration.

Many of the built-in packages, including DBMS_OUTPUT, DBMS_PIPE, and DBMS_SQL, do not assert WNPS or RNPS, so their use in SQL stored functions is necessarily limited.

Column/function name precedence

If your function has the same name as a table column in your SELECT statement and the function has no parameter, then the column takes precedence over the function. To force the RDBMS to resolve the name to your function, prepend the schema name to it:

```
CREATE TABLE emp(new_sal NUMBER ...);
CREATE FUNCTION new_sal RETURN NUMBER IS ...;

SELECT new_sal FROM emp;        -- Resolves to column.
SELECT scott.new_sal FROM emp;-- Resolves to
                                  function.
```

Oracle8 Objects

In Oracle8, an *object type* combines attributes (data structures) and methods (functions and procedures) into a single programming construct. The object type construct allows programmers to defined their own reusable datatypes for use in PL/SQL programs and table and column definitions.

An instance of an object type is an *object* in the same way that variables are instances of scalar types. Objects are either *persistent* (stored in the database) or *transient* (stored only in PL/SQL variables). Objects can be stored in a database as a row in a table (a row object) or as a column in a table. A table of row objects can be created with syntax such as this:

```
CREATE TABLE table_name OF object_type;
```

When stored in the database as a row object, the object (row) has an OID (Object IDentifier) that is unique throughout the database.

Object Types

An object type has two parts: the specification and the body. The specification is required and contains the attributes and method specifications. The syntax for creating the object type specification is:

```
CREATE [OR REPLACE] TYPE obj_type_name
[AUTHID CURRENT_USER | DEFINER] -- Oracle8i
AS OBJECT (
    attribute_name datatype,...,
    [MEMBER | STATIC PROCEDURE | FUNCTION
        program_spec],
    [ORDER | MAP MEMBER FUNCTION
        comparison_function_spec],
    [PRAGMA RESTRICT_REFERENCES(program_name,
        purities)]
);
```

All attribute specifications must appear before all method specifications. Object attributes, like variables, are declared with a name and a datatype. The name can be any legal identifier. Attribute datatypes can be any SQL datatype except LONG, LONG RAW, NCHAR, NVARCHAR2, NCLOB, ROWID, and UROWID. Attributes cannot have datatypes unique to PL/SQL such as BOOLEAN.

Member function and procedure headers are listed in the object type specification in a comma-delimited list. Unlike in a package specification, commas (not semicolons) terminate the object type program specifications. To support object comparisons and sorting, the type can optionally include one comparison method—either ORDER or MAP.

Member programs can assert purity with the RESTRICT_REFERENCES pragma. (See the earlier "Syntax for Calling Stored Functions in SQL" section for more information on this pragma.) Member methods can be overloaded in object types following the same rules as function and procedure overloading in packages.

The syntax for creating the object type body is:

```
CREATE [OR REPLACE] TYPE BODY obj_type_name
AS OBJECT (
       [MEMBER | STATIC PROCEDURE | FUNCTION
           program_body;]
    [ORDER | MAP MEMBER FUNCTION
       comparison_function_body;]
);
```

The keyword STATIC is new starting with Oracle8*i*. Static methods do not use the current SELF object.

Methods

Every object has a default method, a *constructor*, which has the same name as the object type. The constructor *constructs* an instance of the object type from the elements passed to it, and returns the new object. This built-in method:

- Has the same name as the object type
- Is a function that returns an object of that type

- Accepts attributes in named or positional notation
- Must be called with a value (or NULL) for every attribute—there is no DEFAULT clause for object attributes
- Cannot be modified

If you wish to create your own pseudo-constructor, create a STATIC function that returns an object of the corresponding type.

All non-static methods have the built-in parameter SELF, which references the instance of the object. The default mode for the SELF parameter is IN for functions and IN OUT for procedures. SELF can be explicitly declared with a non-default mode.

ORDER and MAP methods establish ordinal positions of objects for non-equality comparisons such as "<" or "between" and for sorting (ORDER BY, GROUP BY, DISTINCT). An ORDER function accepts two parameters: SELF, and another object of the same type. It must return an INTEGER with values of −1, 0, 1, or NULL.

See the following table for a description of these return values.

Return Value	Object Comparison
−1	SELF < second object
0	SELF = second object
1	SELF > second object
NULL	Undefined comparison, i.e., attributes needed for the comparison are NULL

For example, the Senate ranks majority party members higher than non-majority party members and within the majority (or non-majority), by years of service. Here is an example ORDER function incorporating these rules:

```
CREATE TYPE senator_t AS OBJECT (
   majority boolean_t,
   yrs_service NUMBER,
   ORDER MEMBER FUNCTION ranking (other IN
      senator_t)
      RETURN INTEGER  );

CREATE OR REPLACE TYPE BODY senator_t AS
   ORDER MEMBER FUNCTION ranking (other IN
      senator_t)
      RETURN INTEGER
   IS
   BEGIN
      IF SELF.majority.istrue()
         AND other.majority.istrue()
      THEN
         RETURN SIGN(SELF.yrs_service -
            other.yrs_service);
      ELSIF SELF.majority.istrue()
         AND other.majority.isfalse()
      THEN
         RETURN 1;
      ELSIF SELF.majority.isfalse()
         AND other.majority.istrue()
      THEN
         RETURN -1;
      ELSIF SELF.majority.isfalse()
         AND other.majority.isfalse()
      THEN
         RETURN SIGN(SELF.yrs_service -
            other.yrs_service);
      END IF;
   END ranking;
END;
```

A MAP function accepts no parameters and returns a scalar
datatype such as DATE, NUMBER, or VARCHAR2 for which
Oracle already knows a collating sequence. The MAP function translates, or *maps*, each object into a scalar datatype
space that Oracle knows how to compare. When they exist,
MAP methods are often more efficient than ORDER methods and are required for hash joins on the object in SQL.

If no ORDER or MAP function exists for an object type,
SQL, but not PL/SQL, supports only limited equality comparisons of objects. Objects are equal if they are of the
same object type and if each attribute is equal.

Manipulating Objects in PL/SQL and SQL

There are three ways to initialize an object:

1. Using the constructor method

2. Directly assignmening an existing object to a new object

3. Using SELECT INTO or FETCH INTO

Here is an example using each initialization technique:

```
DECLARE
    project_boiler_plate   project_t;
    build_web_site         project_t;

    -- Initialize via constructor.
    new_web_mgr  proj_mgr_t :=
        proj_mgr_t('Ruth', 'Home Office');

    CURSOR template_cur IS
       SELECT VALUE(proj)
         FROM projects
        WHERE project_type = 'TEMPLATE'
          AND  sub_type = 'WEB SITE';
BEGIN
    OPEN template_cur;
    -- Initialize via FETCH INTO.
    FETCH template_cur
        INTO project_boiler_plate;

    -- Initialize via assignment.
    build_web_site := project_boiler_plate;
    ...
```

After an object is initialized, it can be stored in the database, and you can then locate and use that object with the REF, VALUE, and DEREF operators.

The REF operator

REF, short for REFerence, designates a datatype modifier or an operator to retrieve a logical pointer to an object. This pointer encapsulates the OID and can simplify navigation among related database objects.

The syntax for a REF operator is:

```
REF(table_alias_name)
```

For example:

```
SELECT REF(p) FROM pets p WHERE ...
```

A PL/SQL variable can hold a reference to a particular object type:

```
DECLARE
   petref REF Pet_t;
BEGIN
   SELECT REF(p) INTO petref FROM pets p WHERE ...
```

Through deletions, REFs can reference a nonexistent object—called a dangling REF—resulting in a state that can be detected with the IS DANGLING predicate. For example:

```
UPDATE pets
   SET owner_ref = NULL
 WHERE owner_ref IS DANGLING.
```

The VALUE operator

Use the VALUE operator to retrieve a row object as a single object rather than multiple columns. The syntax for the VALUE operator is:

```
VALUE(table_alias_name)
```

For example:

```
SELECT VALUE(p) FROM pets p WHERE ...
```

The DEREF operator

Use the DEREF operator to retrieve the value of an object for which you have a REF. The syntax for the DEREF operator is:

```
DEREF(table_alias_name)
```

For example:

```
DECLARE
   person_ref    REF person_t;
   author        person_t;
BEGIN
   -- Get the ref.
```

```
SELECT REF(p) INTO person_ref
    FROM persons WHERE p.last_name ='Pribyl';

-- Dereference the pointer back to the value.
SELECT DEREF(person_ref) INTO author FROM dual;
...
```

Additionally, Oracle uses an OID internally as a unique key to each object. Like a ROWID, you don't typically use an OID directly.

The following table shows ways of referencing persistent objects.

Scheme	Description	Applications
OID	An opaque, globally unique handle, produced when the object is stored in the database as a table (row) object.	This is the persistent object's handle; it's what REFs point to. Your program never uses it directly.
VALUE	An operator. In SQL, it acts on an object in an object table and returns the object's *contents*. Different from the VALUES keyword found in some INSERT statements.	Allows quasi-normalizing of object-relational databases and joining of object tables using dot navigation. In PL/SQL, REFs serve as input/output variables.
REF	A pointer to an object. May be used within a SQL statement as an operator or in a declaration as a type modifier.	Used when fetching a table (row) object into a variable, or when you need to refer to an object table as an object instead of a list of columns.
DEREF	Reverse pointer lookup for REFs.	Used for retrieving the contents of an object when all you know is its REF.

Changing Object Types

You can add methods, but not attributes, to an object type stored in the database using the ALTER TYPE statement:

```
ALTER TYPE type_name REPLACE AS OBJECT (
   new_object_type_specification
);
```

The only supported change you can make in the new object type specification is to include new methods.

It is also possible to rebuild an object table with different physical storage characteristics by using the built-in procedure DBMS_DDL.ALTER_TABLE_REFERENCEABLE.

The syntax for dropping an object type is:

```
DROP TYPE type_name [FORCE];
```

You can drop only an object type that has not been implemented in a table (or you can drop the tables first). The FORCE option will drop object types even if they have dependencies, but FORCE will irreversibly invalidate any dependent objects such as tables. FORCE does not do a DROP CASCADE.

Collections

There are three types of collections: index-by tables (formerly known as PL/SQL tables), nested tables, and VARRAYs.

Index-by table

Single-dimension, unbounded collections of homogeneous elements available only in PL/SQL, not in the database. Index-by tables are initially sparse; they have nonconsecutive subscripts.

Nested table

Single-dimension, unbounded collections of homogeneous elements available in both PL/SQL and the database as columns or tables. Nested tables are initially dense (they have consecutive subscripts), but can become sparse through deletions.

VARRAYs

Variable-size arrays are single-dimension, bounded collections of homogeneous elements available in both PL/SQL and the database. VARRAYs are never sparse.

Unlike nested tables, their element order is preserved when you store and retrieve them from the database.

The following table compares these similar collection types.

Characteristic	Collection Type		
	Index-by Table	Nested Table	VARRAY
Dimensionality	Single	Single	Single
Usable in SQL?	No	Yes	Yes
Usable as a column datatype in a table?	No	Yes; data stored "out of line" (in a separate table)	Yes; data typically stored "in line" (in the same table)
Uninitialized state	Empty (cannot be NULL); elements are undefined	Atomically null; illegal to reference elements	Atomically null; illegal to reference elements
Initialization	Automatic, when declared	Via constructor, fetch, assignment	Via constructor, fetch, assignment
In PL/SQL, elements referenced by	BINARY_INTEGER (−2,147,483,647 .. 2,147,483,647)	Positive integer between 1 and 2,147483,647	Positive integer between 1 and 2,147483,647
Sparse?	Yes	Initially no; after deletions, yes	No
Bounded?	No	Can be extended	Yes
Can assign a value to any element at any time?	Yes	No; may need to EXTEND first	No; may need to EXTEND first, and cannot EXTEND past the upper bound
Means of extending	Assign value to element with a new subscript	Use built-in EXTEND procedure or TRIM to condense, with no predefined maximum	EXTEND or TRIM, but only up to declared maximum size.

		Collection Type	
Characteristic	Index-by Table	Nested Table	VARRAY
Can be compared for equality?	No	No	No
Elements retain ordinal position and subscript when stored and retrieved from the database	N/A—can't be stored in database	No	Yes

Syntax for Declaring Collection Datatypes

Collections are implemented as TYPEs. Like any programmer-defined type, you must first define the type; then you can declare instances of that type. The TYPE definition can be stored in the database or declared in the PL/SQL program. Each instance of the TYPE is a collection.

The syntax for declaring an index-by table is:

```
TYPE type_name IS TABLE OF element_type [NOT NULL]
INDEX BY BINARY_INTEGER;
```

The syntax for a nested table is:

```
[CREATE [OR REPLACE]] TYPE type_name IS TABLE OF
    element_type [NOT NULL];
```

The syntax for a VARRAY is:

```
[CREATE [OR REPLACE]] TYPE type_name IS VARRAY |
    VARYING ARRAY (max_elements) OF element_type
    [NOT NULL];
```

The CREATE keyword defines the statement to be DDL and indicates that this type will exist in the database. The optional OR REPLACE keywords are used to rebuild an existing type, preserving the privileges. *type_name* is any valid identifier that will be used later to declare the collection. *max_elements* is the maximum size of the VARRAY. *element_type* is the type of the collection's elements. All elements are of a single type, which can be most scalar datatypes, an object type, or a REF object type. If the elements are objects, the object type itself cannot have an attribute that is a collection. Explicitly disallowed collection datatypes are BOOLEAN, NCHAR, NCLOB, NVARCHAR2, REF CURSOR, TABLE, and VARRAY.

NOT NULL indicates that a collection of this type cannot have any null elements. However, the collection can be atomically null (uninitialized).

Initializing Collections

Initializing an index-by table is trivial—simply declaring it also initializes it. Initializing a nested table or VARRAY can be done explicitly, with a constructor, or implicitly with a fetch from the database or a direct assignment of another collection variable.

The constructor is a built-in function with the same name as the collection. It constructs the collection from the elements passed to it. We can create a nested table of colors and initialize it to three elements with a constructor:

```
DECLARE
    TYPE colors_tab_t IS TABLE OF VARCHAR2(30);
    basic_colors colors_tab_t :=

    colors_tab_t('RED','GREEN','BLUE');
BEGIN
```

We can create our nested table of colors and initialize it with a fetch from the database:

```
-- Create the nested table to exist in the database.
CREATE TYPE colors_tab_t IS TABLE OF VARCHAR2(32);

-- Create table with nested table type as column.
CREATE TABLE color_models
(model_type    VARCHAR2(12)
,colors        color_tab_t)
NESTED TABLE colors STORE AS
    color_model_colors_tab;

-- Add some data to the table.
INSERT INTO color_models
```

```
      VALUES('RGB',color_tab_t('RED','GREEN','BLUE'));
   INSERT INTO color_models
      VALUES('CYMK',color_tab_t('CYAN','YELLOW',
         'MAGENTA' 'BLACK'));

   -- Initialize a collection of colors from the table.
   DECLARE
      basic_colors colors_tab_t;
   BEGIN
      SELECT colors INTO basic_colors
        FROM color_models
       WHERE model_type = 'RGB';
   ...
   END;
```

The third initialization technique is by assignment from an existing collection:

```
DECLARE
   basic_colors Color_tab_t :=
      Color_tab_t ('RED','GREEN','BLUE');

   my_colors Color_tab_t;
BEGIN
   my_colors := basic_colors;
   my_colors(2) := 'MUSTARD';
```

Adding and Removing Elements

Elements in an index-by table can be added simply by referencing new subscripts. To add elements to nested tables or VARRAYs, you must first enlarge the collection with the EXTEND function, and then you can assign a value to a new element using one of the methods described in the previous section.

Use the DELETE function to remove an element in a nested table regardless of its position. The TRIM function can also be used to remove elements, but only from the end of a collection. To avoid unexpected results, do not use both DELETE and TRIM on the same collection.

Collection Pseudo-Functions

There are several psuedo-functions defined for collections. They include THE, CAST, MULTISET, and TABLE.

THE

Maps a single column's value in a single row into a virtual database table. Syntactically, this is similar to an inline view, where a subquery is used in the FROM clause.

```
SELECT VALUE(c)
  FROM THE(SELECT colors
             FROM color_models
            WHERE model_type = 'RGB') c;
```

The pseudo-function THE will work in Oracle8*i* but its use is discouraged. Use the 8*i* TABLE() function instead.

CAST

Maps a collection of one type to a collection of another type.

```
SELECT column_value
FROM THE(SELECT CAST(colors AS color_tab_t)
           FROM color_models_a
          WHERE model_type ='RGB');
```

MULTISET

Maps a database table to a collection. With MULTISET and CAST, you can retrieve rows from a database table as a collection-typed column.

```
SELECT b.genus ,b.species,
       CAST(MULTISET(SELECT bh.country
                       FROM bird_habitats bh
                      WHERE bh.genus = b.genus
                        AND bh.species = b.species)
            AS country_tab_t)
FROM birds b;
```

TABLE

Maps a collection to a database table; the inverse of MULTISET.

```
SELECT *
  FROM color_models c
 WHERE 'RED' IN (SELECT * FROM TABLE(c.colors));
```

In Oracle8*i* PL/SQL, you can use TABLE() to unnest a transient collection:

```
DECLARE
   birthdays Birthdate_t :=
```

```
        Birthdate_t('24-SEP-1984', '19-JUN-1993');
    BEGIN
      FOR the_rec IN
        (SELECT COLUMN_VALUE
            FROM TABLE(CAST(birthdays AS Birthdate_t)))
```

Collection Methods

There are a number of built-in functions (methods) defined for all collections. These methods are called with dot notation:

```
collection_name.method_name[(parameters)]
```

The methods are described in the following table.

Collection Method	Description
COUNT function	Returns the current number of elements in the collection.
DELETE [(i[,j])] procedure	Removes element *i* or elements *i* through *j* from a nested table or index-by table. When called with no parameters, removes all elements in the collection. Reduces the COUNT if the element is not already DELETEd. Does not apply to VARRAYs.
EXISTS(i) function	Returns TRUE or FALSE to indicate whether element *i* exists. If the collection is an uninitialized nested table or VARRAY, returns FALSE.
EXTEND [(n[,i])] procedure	Appends *n* elements to a collection, initializing them to the value of element *i*. *n* is optional and defaults to 1.
FIRST function	Returns the smallest index in use. Returns NULL when applied to empty initialized collections.
LAST function	Returns the largest index in use. Returns NULL when applied to empty initialized collections.
LIMIT function	Returns the maximum number of allowed elements in a VARRAY. Returns NULL for index-by tables and nested tables.
PRIOR (i) function	Return the index immediately before element *i*. Returns NULL if *i* is less than or equal to FIRST.

Collection Method	Description
NEXT (i) function	Return the index immediately after element *i*. Returns NULL if *i* is greater than or equal to COUNT.
TRIM [(n)] procedure	Removes *n* elements at the end of the collection with the largest index. *n* is optional and defaults to 1. If *n* is NULL, TRIM does nothing. Index-by tables cannot be TRIMmed.

The EXISTS function returns a BOOLEAN and all other functions return BINARY_INTEGER. All parameters are of the BINARY_INTEGER type.

Only EXISTS can be used on uninitialized nested tables or VARRAYs. Other methods applied to these atomically null collections will raise the COLLECTION_IS_NULL exception.

DELETE and TRIM both remove elements from a nested table, but TRIM also removes the placeholder, while DELETE does not. This behavior may be confusing, since TRIM can remove previously DELETED elements.

Here is an example of some collection methods in use:

```
DECLARE
   TYPE colors_tab_t IS TABLE OF VARCHAR2(30);
   my_list colors_tab_t :=
      colors_tab_t('RED','GREEN','BLUE');
   element BINARY_INTEGER;
BEGIN
   DBMS_OUTPUT.PUT_LINE('my_list has '
      ||my_list.COUNT||' elements');
   my_list.DELETE(2); -- delete element two
   DBMS_OUTPUT.PUT_LINE('my_list has '
      ||my_list.COUNT||' elements');

   FOR element IN my_list.FIRST..my_list.LAST
   LOOP
      IF my_list.EXISTS(element)
      THEN
         DBMS_OUTPUT.PUT_LINE(my_list(element)
            || ' Prior= '||my_list.PRIOR(element)
            || ' Next= ' ||my_list.NEXT(element));
      ELSE
         DBMS_OUTPUT.PUT_LINE('Element '|| element
```

```
                ||' deleted. Prior= '||my_
                    list.PRIOR(element)
                || ' Next= '||my_list.NEXT(element));
        END IF;
      END LOOP;
    END;
```

This example gives the output:

```
my_list has 3 elements
my_list has 2 elements
RED Prior=  Next= 3
Element 2 deleted. Prior= 1 Next= 3
BLUE Prior= 1 Next=
```

Privileges

As with other TYPEs in the database, you need the EXE-
CUTE privilege on that TYPE in order to use a collection
type created by another schema (user account) in the
database.

Bulk Binds (Oracle8i)

Starting with Oracle8*i*, you can use collections to improve
the performance of SQL operations executed iteratively by
using bulk binds. *Bulk binds* reduce the number of round-
trips that must be made between a client application and
the database. Two PL/SQL language constructs implement
bulk binds: FORALL and BULK COLLECT INTO.

The syntax for the FORALL statement is:

```
FORALL bulk_index IN lower_bound..upper_bound
    sql_statement;
```

bulk_index can be used only in the *sql_statement* and only
as a collection index (subscript). When PL/SQL processes
this statement, the whole collection, instead of each individual collection element, is sent to the database server for
processing. To delete all the accounts in the collection inac-
tives from the table ledger, do this:

```
FORALL i IN inactives.FIRST..inactives.LAST
    DELETE FROM ledger WHERE acct_no = inactives(i);
```

The syntax for the BULK COLLECT INTO clause is:

```
BULK COLLECT INTO collection_name_list;
```

where *collection_name_list* is a comma-delimited list of collections, one for each column in the SELECT. As of Oracle8*i*, collections of records cannot be a target of a BULK COLLECT INTO clause. However, 8*i* does support retrieving a set of typed objects and "bulk collecting" them into a collection of objects.

The BULK COLLECT INTO clause can be used in SELECT INTO, FETCH INTO, or RETURNING INTO statements. For example:

```
DECLARE
    TYPE vendor_name_tab IS TABLE OF
        vendors.name%TYPE;
    TYPE vendor_term_tab IS TABLE OF
        vendors.terms%TYPE;
    v_names vendor_name_tab;
    v_terms vendor_term_tab;
BEGIN
    SELECT name, terms
        BULK COLLECT INTO v_names, v_terms
        FROM vendors
        WHERE terms < 30;
    ...
END;
```

The next function deletes employees in an input list of departments, and the (Oracle8) SQL RETURNING clause returns a list of deleted employees:

```
FUNCTION whack_emps_by_dept (deptlist dlist_t)
RETURN enolist_t
IS
    enolist enolist_t;
BEGIN
    FORALL adept IN deptlist.FIRST..deptlist.LAST
        DELETE FROM emp WHERE deptno IN
            deptlist(adept)
            RETURNING empno BULK COLLECT INTO enolist;
    RETURN Enolist;
END;
```

You can use the SQL%BULK_ROWCOUNT cursor attribute for bulk bind operations. It is like an index-by table containing the number of rows affected by the executions of the bulk bound statements. The *n*th element of SQL%BULK_ROWCOUNT contains the number of rows affected by *n*th execution of the SQL statement. For example:

```
FORALL i IN inactives.FIRST..inactives.LAST
   DELETE FROM ledger WHERE acct_no = inactives(i);
FOR counter IN inactives.FIRST..inactives.LAST
LOOP
   IF SQL%BULK_ROWCOUNT(counter) = 0
   THEN
      DBMS_OUTPUT.PUT_LINE('No rows deleted for '||
         counter);
   END IF;
END LOOP;
```

You cannot pass SQL%BULK_ROWCOUNT as a parameter to another program, or use an aggregate assignment to another collection. %ROWCOUNT contains a summation of all %BULK_ROWCOUNT elements. %FOUND and %NOT-FOUND reflect only the last execution of the SQL statement.

External Procedures

External procedures provide a mechanism for calling out to a non-database program, such as a DLL under NT or a shared library under Unix. Every session calling an external procedure will have its own *extproc* process started by the listener. This extproc process is started with the first call to the external procedure and terminates when the session exits. The shared library needs to have a corresponding library created for it in the database.

Creating an External Procedure

The following are the steps you need to follow in order to create an external procedure.

Set up the listener

External procedures require a listener. If you are running a Net8 listener, it can be used as the extproc listener as well. See the *Oracle8 Administrators' Guide* or the *Net8 Administrators' Guide* for the details on configuring your listener.

Identify or create the shared library or DLL

This step has nothing to do with PL/SQL or the database. You must write your own C routines and link them into a shared library/DLL or use an existing library's functions or procedures. In the simple example below, we will use the existing random number generating calls available from the operating system.

Create the library in the database

Create a library in the database for the shared library or DLL using the CREATE LIBRARY statement:

```
CREATE [OR REPLACE] LIBRARY library_name IS | AS
    'absolute_path_and_file';
```

To remove libraries from the database, you use the DROP LIBRARY statement:

```
DROP LIBRARY library_name;
```

To call out to the C runtime library's *rand* function, you don't have to code any C routines at all, since the call is already linked into a shared library, and because its arguments are directly type-mappable to PL/SQL. If the rand function is in the standard */lib/libc.so* shared library, as on Solaris, you would issue the following CREATE LIBRARY statement:

```
CREATE OR REPLACE LIBRARY libc_l AS
    '/lib/libc.so';  -- References C runtime library.
```

This is the typical corresponding statement for NT:

```
CREATE OR REPLACE LIBRARY libc_l AS
    'C:\WINNT\SYSTEM32\CRTDLL.DLL';
```

Create the PL/SQL wrapper for the external procedure

The syntax for the wrapper procedure is:

```
CREATE [OR REPLACE] PROCEDURE proc_name
    [parm_list]
AS|IS EXTERNAL
    LIBRARY library_name
    [NAME external_name]
    [LANGUAGE language_name]
    [CALLING STANDARD  C | PASCAL]
    [WITH CONTEXT]
    [PARAMETERS (external_parameter_list)];
```

The following are the syntactic elements defined:

proc_name

The name of the wrapper procedure.

library_name

The name of the library created with the CREATE LIBRARY statement.

external_name

The name of the external routine as it appears in the library. It defaults to the wrapper package name. PL/SQL package names are usually saved in uppercase, so the *external_name* may need to be enclosed in double quotes to preserve case.

language_name

The language that the external routine was written in. It defaults to C.

CALLING STANDARD

The calling standard, which defaults to C. The Pascal calling standard reverses the order of the parameters, and the called routine is responsible for popping the parameters off the stack.

WITH CONTEXT

Used to pass a context pointer to the external routine, so it can make OCI calls back to the database.

PARAMETERS

Identify the *external_parameter_list*, which is a comma-delimited list containing the position and datatype of parameters that get passed to the external routine. For more details on the *external_parameter_list*, see the next section, "Parameters".

The wrapper PL/SQL function or procedure is usually in a package. Using the preceding random number generator example, we could create the wrapper package as follows:

```
CREATE OR REPLACE PACKAGE random_utl
AS
    FUNCTION rand RETURN PLS_INTEGER;
    PRAGMA RESTRICT_
REFERENCES(rand,WNDS,RNDS,WNPS,RNPS);

    PROCEDURE srand (seed IN PLS_INTEGER);
    PRAGMA RESTRICT_
REFERENCES(srand,WNDS,RNDS,WNPS,RNPS);
END random_utl;

CREATE PACKAGE BODY random_utl
AS
    FUNCTION rand RETURN PLS_INTEGER
    IS
        EXTERNAL        -- Keyword to indicate external
                           routine.
        LIBRARY libc_l -- The library created above.
        NAME "rand"    -- Function name in the
                          library.
        LANGUAGE C;    -- Language of routine.

    PROCEDURE srand (seed IN PLS_INTEGER)
    IS
        EXTERNAL LIBRARY libc_l
        NAME "srand"   -- Name is lowercase in this
                          library.
        LANGUAGE C
        PARAMETERS (seed ub4); --Map to unsigned
                                  4byte.
INT
END random_utl;
```

To use this external random number function, we simply call the package procedure *srand* to seed the generator, then the package function *rand* to get random numbers:

```
DECLARE
    random_nbr   PLS_INTEGER;
    seed         PLS_INTEGER;
BEGIN
    SELECT TO_CHAR(SYSDATE,'SSSSS') INTO seed
        FROM dual;

    random_utl.srand(seed);  -- Seed the generator.

    random_nbr := random_utl.rand; -- Get the number.
    DBMS_OUTPUT.PUT_LINE('number='||random_nbr);

    random_nbr := random_utl.rand; -- Get the number.
    DBMS_OUTPUT.PUT_LINE('number='||random_nbr);
END;
```

You can generate random numbers without the complexity or overhead of an external call by using the built-in package DBMS_RANDOM. To learn more about DBMS_RANDOM and other built-ins, see O'Reilly's books *Oracle Built-in Packages* and *Oracle PL/SQL Built-ins Pocket Reference*.

Parameters

When it comes to passing PL/SQL variables to C variables, we encounter many inconsistencies. For example, PL/SQL supports nullity, while C does not; PL/SQL can have variables in different character sets, while C cannot; and the datatypes in PL/SQL do not directly map to C datatypes.

The PARAMETERS clause specifies the external parameter list, a comma-delimited list containing parameters. The syntax for each parameter in the list is:

```
CONTEXT | RETURN | parameter_name [property]
    [BY REFERENCE] [external_datatype]
```

The keyword CONTEXT indicates the position in the parameter list at which the context pointer will be passed. It is required if the WITH CONTEXT clause is being used to pass a context pointer to the called program. By convention, CONTEXT appears as the first parameter in the external parameter list. If CONTEXT is used, the *property,* BY REFERENCE, and *external_datatype* optional sections are invalid.

The keyword RETURN indicates that the descriptions are for the return value from the external routine. By default, RETURN is passed by value. You can use the keywords BY REFERENCE to pass by reference (use pointers).

parameter_name is a PL/SQL formal parameter name. By default, IN formal parameters are passed by value. You can use the key words BY REFERENCE to pass by reference (as a pointer). IN OUT and OUT formal parameters are always passed by reference.

property breaks out further to the general Oracle8 syntax:

```
INDICATOR | LENGTH | MAXLEN | CHARSETID| CHARSETFORM
```

The general Oracle8*i* syntax is:

```
INDICATOR [STRUCT | TDO ] | LENGTH | MAXLEN |
    CHARSETID | CHARSETFORM | SELF
```

INDICATOR indicates whether the corresponding parameter is NULL. In the C program, if the indicator equals the constant OCI_IND_NULL, the parameter is NULL. If the indicator equals the constant OCI_IND_NOTNULL, the indicator is not NULL. For IN parameters, INDICATOR is passed by value (by default). For IN OUT, OUT, and RETURN parameters, INDICATOR is passed by reference.

In Oracle8*i*, you can pass a user-defined type to an external procedure. To do so, you will typically pass three parameters: the actual object value; a TDO (Type Descriptor Object) parameter as defined in C by the Oracle Type Translator; and an INDICATOR STRUCT parameter, to designate whether the object is NULL.

LENGTH and MAXLEN can be used to pass the current and maximum length of strings or RAWs. For IN parameters, LENGTH is passed by value (by default). For IN OUT, OUT, and RETURN parameters, LENGTH is passed by reference. MAXLEN is not valid for IN parameters. For IN OUT, OUT, and RETURN parameters, MAXLEN is passed by reference and is read-only.

CHARSETID and CHARSETFORM are used to support NLS character sets. They are the same as the OCI attributes OCI_ATTR_CHARSET_ID and OCI_ATTR_CHARSET_FORM. For IN parameters, CHARSETID and CHARSETFORM are passed by value (by default) and are read-only. For IN OUT, OUT, and RETURN parameters, CHARSETID and CHARSETFORM are passed by reference and are read-only.

SELF is used if an object member function is implemented as a callout instead of a PL/SQL routine.

Java Language Integration

In Oracle8*i*, Java™ programmers can write server-side classes that invoke SQL and PL/SQL using standard JDBC™ or SQLJ calls. PL/SQL programmers can call server-side Java methods by writing a PL/SQL cover or *call spec* for Java using Oracle DDL.

Server-side Java in Oracle may be faster than PL/SQL for compute-intensive programs, but not as nimble for database access. PL/SQL is much more efficient for database-intensive routines because, unlike Java, it doesn't have to pay the overhead for converting SQL datatypes for use inside the stored program. Oracle programmers will want to continue to use PL/SQL for programs that perform a lot of database I/O, and use Java for the best raw computation performance.

The first step in creating a *Java stored procedure* (JSP) is writing or otherwise obtaining functional Java code. Having source code is not necessary, though, so you can use class libraries from third parties. The classes must, however, meet the following requirements:

- Methods published to SQL and PL/SQL must be declared static. PL/SQL has no mechanisms for instantiating non-static Java classes.

- The classes must not issue any GUI calls (for example, to AWT) at runtime.

If you write your own JSP, and it needs to connect to the database for access to tables or stored procedures, use standard JDBC and/or SQLJ calls in your code. Many JDBC and SQLJ reference materials are available to provide assistance in calling SQL or PL/SQL from Java, but be sure to review the Oracle-specific documentation that ships with Oracle8*i*.

Once you have the Java class in hand, either in source or *.class* file format, the next step is loading it into the database. Oracle's *loadjava* command-line utility is a convenient way to accomplish the load. Refer to Oracle's documentation for further assistance with *loadjava*.

The third step is to create a call spec for the Java method, specifying the AS LANGUAGE JAVA clause of the CREATE command. You may create a function or procedure cover as appropriate.

Finally, you may grant execute privileges on the new JSP using GRANT EXECUTE, and PL/SQL routines can now call the JSP as if it were another PL/SQL module.

Example

Let's write a simple "Hello, World" JSP that will accept an argument:

```
package oreilly.plsquick.demos;

public class Hello {
    public static String sayIt (String toWhom) {
        return "Hello, " + toWhom + "!";
    }
}
```

Saved in a file called *Hello.java*, we can load the source code directly into Oracle. Doing so will automatically compile the code. A simple form of the *loadjava* command:

```
loadjava -user scott/tiger -oci8 oreilly/plsquick/
    demos/Hello.java
```

The *Hello.java* file follows the Java file placement convention for packages and so exists in a subdirectory named *oreilly/plsquick/demos*.

Now we can fire up our favorite SQL interpreter, connect as
SCOTT/TIGER, and create the call spec for the Hello.sayIt()
method:

```
CREATE FUNCTION hello_there (to_whom IN VARCHAR2)
    RETURN VARCHAR2
    AS LANGUAGE JAVA
    NAME 'oreilly.plsquick.demos.Hello.sayIt
      (java.lang.String) return java.lang.String';
/
```

Now we can call our function very easily:

```
BEGIN
    DBMS_OUTPUT.PUT_LINE(hello_there('world'));
END;
/
```

And we get:

```
Hello, world!
```

as the expected output.

Publishing Java to PL/SQL

To write a call spec, use the AS LANGUAGE JAVA clause in
a CREATE statement. The syntax for this clause is:

```
{ IS | AS } LANGUAGE JAVA
    NAME 'method_fullname [ (type_fullname,... ]
      [ return type_fullname ]'
```

method_fullname is the package-qualified name of the Java
class and method. It is case-sensitive and uses dots to separate parts of the package full name. *type_fullname* is the
package-qualified name of the Java datatype.

Notice that a simple string, not an SQL name, follows the
NAME keyword.

Type mapping follows most JDBC rules regarding the legal
mapping of SQL types to Java types. Oracle extensions exist
for Oracle-specific datatypes.

Most datatype mappings are relatively straightforward, but
passing Oracle8 objects of a user-defined type is harder
than one would think. Oracle provides a JPublisher tool

that generates the Java required to encapsulate an Oracle8 object and its corresponding REF. Refer to Oracle's JPublisher documentation for guidelines on usage.

The AS LANGUAGE JAVA clause is the same whether you are using Java as a standalone JSP, the implementation of a packaged program, or the body of an object type method. For example, here is the complete syntax for creating JSPs as PL/SQL-callable functions or procedures:

```
CREATE [OR REPLACE]
{   PROCEDURE procedure_name [(param[, param]...)]
    | FUNCTION function_name [(param[, param]...)]
        RETURN sql_type
}
[AUTHID {DEFINER | CURRENT_USER}]
[PARALLEL_ENABLE]
[DETERMINISTIC]
{ IS | AS } LANGUAGE JAVA
    NAME 'method_fullname [ (type_fullname,... ]
        [ return type_fullname ]'
```

When using Java as the implementation of a packaged procedure or function, Oracle allows you to place the Java call spec in either the package specification (where the call spec substitutes for the subprogram specification) or in the package body (where the call spec substitutes for the subprogram body).

Similarly, when using JSPs in object type methods, the Java call spec can substitute for either the object type method specification or its body.

Note that Java functions typically map to PL/SQL functions, but Java functions declared void map to PL/SQL procedures. Also, you will quickly learn that mistakes in mapping PL/SQL parameters to Java parameters become evident only at runtime.

Data Dictionary

To learn what Java library units are available in your schema, look in the USER_OBJECTS data dictionary view where the *object_type* is like 'JAVA%'. If you see a Java class with

---

INVALID status, it has not yet been successfully resolved. Note that the names of the Java source library units need not match the names of the classes they produce.

As of press time, there is no apparent way to discover which stored programs are implemented as Java stored procedures. You can look in the USER_SOURCE view for named programs that contain the source text 'AS LANGUAGE JAVA', but that may not yield accurate results. The USER_DEPENDENCIES view does not track the relationship between PL/SQL cover programs and their underlying Java class.

Even if you have loaded the Java source code into the database, there is no supported way of retrieving the source from the data dictionary.

More Titles from O'Reilly

Oracle

Oracle PL/SQL Programming, 2nd Edition

By Steven Feuerstein with Bill Pribyl
2nd Edition September 1997
1,028 pages, Includes diskette
ISBN 1-56592-335-9

The first edition of *Oracle PL/SQL Programming* quickly
became an indispensable reference for PL/SQL developers.
This new edition covers Oracle8 and includes chapters on
Oracle8 object types, object views, collections, and external
procedures. It also covers new data types and functions,
and contains new chapters on tuning, tracing, and debugging PL/SQL programs.
The companion diskette contains an online Windows-based tool offering access
to more than 100 files of source code and documentation prepared by the authors.

Advanced Oracle PL/SQL *Programming with Packages*

By Steven Feuerstein
1st Edition Oct.1996
690 pages, Includes diskette
ISBN 1-56592-238-7

This book explains the best way to construct packages, a
powerful part of Oracle's PL/SQL procedural language that
can dramatically improve your programming productivity
and code quality, while preparing you for object-oriented
development in Oracle technology. It comes with PL/Vision
software, a library of PL/SQL packages developed by the author, and takes you
behind the scenes as it examines how and why the PL/Vision packages were
implemented the way they were.

O'REILLY®

Oracle

Oracle Security

By Marlene Theriault & William Heney
1st Edition October 1998
446 pages
ISBN 1-56592-450-9

This book covers the field of Oracle security from simple to complex. It describes basic RDBMS security features (e.g., passwords, profiles, roles, privileges, synonyms) and includes many practical strategies for securing an Oracle system, developing auditing and backup plans, and using the Oracle Enterprise Manager and Oracle Security Server. Also touches on advanced security features, such as encryption, Trusted Oracle, and Internet and Web protection.

Oracle Design

By Dave Ensor & Ian Stevenson
1st Edition March 1997
546 pages
ISBN 1-56592-268-9

This book looks thoroughly at the field of Oracle relational database design, an often neglected area of Oracle, but one that has an enormous impact on the ultimate power and performance of a system. Focuses on both database and code design, including such special design areas as data models, enormalization, the use of keys and indexes, temporal data, special architectures (client/server, distributed database, parallel processing), and data warehouses.

Oracle

Oracle Built-In Packages

By Steven Feuerstein
1st Edition March 1998
600 pages, Includes diskette
ISBN 1-56592-375-8

Oracle's built-in packages dramatically extend the power of the PL/SQL language, but few developers know how to use them effectively. This book is a complete reference to all of the built-ins, including those new to Oracle8. The enclosed diskette includes an online tool that provides easy access to the many files of source code and documentation developed by the authors.

Oracle Performance Tuning, 2nd Edition

By Mark Gurry & Peter Corrigan
2nd Edition November 1996
964 pages, Includes diskette
ISBN 1-56592-237-9

Performance tuning is crucial in any modern relational database management system. The first edition of this book became a classic for developers and DBAs. This edition offers 400 pages of new material on new Oracle features, including parallel server, parallel query, Oracle Performance Pack, disk striping and mirroring, RAID, MPPs, SMPs, distributed databases, backup and recovery, and much more.

O'REILLY®

TO ORDER: **800-998-9938** • order@oreilly.com • http://www.oreilly.com/
OUR PRODUCTS ARE AVAILABLE AT A BOOKSTORE OR SOFTWARE STORE NEAR YOU.
FOR INFORMATION: **800-998-9938** • **707-829-0515** • info@oreilly.com

Oracle

Oracle8 Design Tips

By Dave Ensor & Ian Stevenson
1st Edition September 1997
130 pages
ISBN 1-56592-361-8

The newest version of the Oracle DBMS, Oracle8, offers some dramatically different features from previous versions, including better scalability, reliability, and security; an object-relational model; additional datatypes; and more. To get peak performance out of an Oracle8 system, databases and code need to be designed with these new features in mind. This small book tells Oracle designers and developers just what they need to know to use the Oracle8 features to best advantage.

Oracle Scripts

By Brian Lomasky & David C. Kreines
1st Edition May 1998
200 pages, Includes CD-ROM
ISBN 1-56592-438-X

A powerful toolset for Oracle DBAs and developers, these scripts will simplify everyday tasks—monitoring databases, protecting against data loss, improving security and performance, and helping to diagnose problems and repair databases in emergencies. The accompanying CD-ROM contains complete source code and additional monitoring and tuning software.

Oracle PL/SQL Built-ins Pocket Reference

By Steven Feuerstein, John Beresniewicz & Chip Dawes
1st Edition October 1998
78 pages, ISBN 1-56592-456-8

This companion to Steven Feuerstein's bestselling *Oracle PL/SQL Programming* and *Oracle Built-in Packages* provides quick-reference information on how to call Oracle's built-in functions and packages, including those new to Oracle8. It shows how to call all types of functions (numeric, character, date, conversion, large object [LOB], and miscellaneous) and packages (e.g., DBMS_SQL, DBMS_OUTPUT).

O'REILLY®

TO ORDER: **800-998-9938** • order@oreilly.com • http://www.oreilly.com/
OUR PRODUCTS ARE AVAILABLE AT A BOOKSTORE OR SOFTWARE STORE NEAR YOU.
FOR INFORMATION: **800-998-9938** • **707-829-0515** • info@oreilly.com